LAROUSSE

POCKET GUIDE TO

BRITISH HISTORY

Editor
Min Lee

Assistant Editors
Angela Cran
Clare Currie

LAROUSSE

LAROUSSE
Larousse plc
7 Hopetoun Crescent
Edinburgh EH7 4AY

First published by Larousse plc 1995
Reprinted 1997

A CIP catalogue record for this book
is available from the British Library

ISBN 0–7523–0033–4

Typeset by Selwood Systems, Midsomer Norton
Printed and bound in Great Britain by
Caledonian International Book Manufacturing Ltd, Glasgow

Contents

Introduction

The *Larousse Pocket Guide to British History* has been drawn from the very large reference database which is the source for titles in the Larousse, Chambers and Kingfisher imprints.

The most interesting dates and facts have been extracted from this database to give an overview of the movement of British history from earliest times to the present day.

The information is set out by century, and under the heading of each year. The reader is presented with the births and deaths of significant individuals, and a selection of the most important events to occur in that year. A comprehensive index allows the user to follow particular people or events and find all references to them.

In addition, there are useful lists at the end of the book, for example of rulers and of explorers, which bring related events together.

The very clear presentation makes this book an ideal quick reference for anyone wanting to find out the essential facts about British history, whatever the level of interest.

BC

5000

★ EVENTS   (c.) Rising sea level severs last land bridge between
    Britain and mainland Europe.

3200

★ EVENTS   (c.) First houses built in Skara Brae, in Orkney,
    Scotland.

3000

★ EVENTS   (c.) Stonehenge (first stage) constructed, on
    Salisbury Plain, England. A complex configuration of stones
    of various types and sizes, it is unclear what the true purpose
    of Stonehenge is; most probably linked to worship.

2300

★ EVENTS   (c.) The settlement at Skara Brae is abandoned,
    intact, when it is engulfed by a sand storm. The villagers
    leave behind all the paraphernalia of everyday life which is
    later discovered by archaeologists.

2000

★ EVENTS   (c.) Beginning of the Bronze Age.

    (c.) Construction of Stonehenge (second stage) begins in
    England.

1900

★ EVENTS   (c.) 24 standing stones are erected at Cairnpapple
    Hill, Lothian, Scotland, and the hill is used for ritual worship
    until the advent of Christianity.

1100

★ EVENTS   (c.) Flag Fen, near Peterborough, established as
    centre of religious cult activity.

325

★ EVENTS   (c.) Probably the earliest documented reference to
Britain and Ireland is made by Pytheas of Massilia, when he
refers to the 'Pretanic' (Britannic) isles.

55

★ EVENTS   (c.) Roman invasion of Britain begins with the first
expedition of Julius Caesar.

54

★ EVENTS   (c.) Second stage of Roman invasion of Britain;
British army crushed.

20

★ EVENTS   (c.) Tincommius becomes King of the Atrebates,
ruling a territory around Hampshire.

10

★ EVENTS   Tincommius of the Atrebates is deposed by his
tribesmen and succeeded by his brother Eppilus.

1

★ EVENTS   Eppilus is, in turn, deposed and the Kingship of the
Atrebates is seized by Verica.

AD
1st Century

5

★ EVENTS   Cymbeline is recognized by Rome as King of Britain.

20

★ EVENTS   (c.) Eppilus, deposed king of the Atrebates, is forced out of exile in Kent by Cymbeline, ruler of south-east England.

41

★ EVENTS   (c.) Planned invasion of Britain by Roman Emperor Gaius (Caligula) peters out.

42

★ EVENTS   (c.) Verica, King of the Atrebates, is ousted, as were his two predecessors.

43

★ EVENTS   Roman invasion of Britain (to 44) ordered by Emperor Claudius. England fortifies its hillforts in response, although some British rulers immediately ally with the Romans. In the course of the campaign many of southern England's hillforts are overthrown and the tribes of the Catuvellauni, Trinovantes and Cantiaci form a defensive league based in Colchester.

47

★ EVENTS   Britain to the Severn in the west and the Trent in the North is now under Roman rule.

48

★ EVENTS   Despite the apparent ease of the Roman invasion so far, the tribes of the Catuvellauni, Trinovantes and Cantiaci continue to resist fiercely under the leadership of Caractacus (or Caratacus), leading to much bloodshed.

49

★ EVENTS   Caractacus pushes forward into Wales.
Colchester is founded by the Romans.

50

★ EVENTS   (c.) London is founded by the Romans.
Caractacus is defeated and seeks refuge with the tribe of the Brigantes.

51

★ EVENTS   Caractacus is betrayed by the Brigantes, handed over to the Romans and imprisoned in Rome.

58

★ EVENTS   The Romans extend their ambitions in Britain to the conquest of the whole island.

61

★ EVENTS   (c.) British queen Boudicca (Boadicea) of the Celtic Iceni tribe leads a revolt against the Romans after their invasion of her East Anglian territory. Up to 70,000 Romans die.

62

★ EVENTS   Boudicca is defeated and poisons herself to avoid capture.

76

★ EVENTS   The Emperor Hadrian is born.

78

★ EVENTS   The Romans strive to conquer northern Britain under the leadership of Gnaeus Julius Agricola.

80

★ EVENTS   Roman conquests expand as far as the Forth and Clyde.

84

★ EVENTS   Romans under Agricola decisively defeat the Scots tribes, inflicting 10,000 casualties on them in battle at Mons Graupius.

2nd Century

100

★ EVENTS   (c.) Temporary Roman loss of control of Scotland.

117

★ EVENTS   Hadrian is crowned Roman emperor.

122

★ EVENTS   (c.) Construction of Hadrian's Wall (to 126) to defend Roman possessions.

138

★ EVENTS   Emperor Hadrian dies.

140

★ EVENTS   Beginning of the Antonine advance into Scotland.

142

★ EVENTS   Construction of the Forth–Clyde Antonine Wall.

196

★ EVENTS   Roman control of the northern frontier lapses as Clodius Albinus withdraws his forces from Britain to focus upon his attempts to become emperor.

3rd Century

208

⭐ EVENTS   Roman Emperor Septimius Severus personally oversees the re-conquest of Scotland.

274

⭐ EVENTS   Britain becomes subject to direct rule from Rome.

287

⭐ EVENTS   The commander of the Roman fleet in Britain, Carausius, breaks from Roman rule and establishes an independent British empire.

293

⭐ EVENTS   Carausius, rebel Roman commander, is killed by his former ally Allectus.

296

⭐ EVENTS   Constanius Chlorus arrives in Britain with a Roman force to resume the conquest begun by Septimius Severus.

4th Century

306

⭐ EVENTS   Constantine I, the Great, proclaimed emperor at York.

363

⭐ EVENTS   Britain subject to repeated attacks by the Saxons.

367

⭐ EVENTS   Onslaught of Barbarian raiders. Picts, Scots and Saxons successfully attack the Romans.

369

★ EVENTS   Barbarians are quelled and Roman authority re-
established.

The Scots and the Picts are expelled from Roman Britain by
Theodosius.

382

★ EVENTS   Picts defeated in battle by the Romans under Magnus
Maximus, the military commander of Britain.

383

★ EVENTS   Magnus Maximus revolts against Rome (to 388), but
is eventually defeated.

5th Century

401

★ EVENTS   (c.) Roman legions begin to vacate Britain and local
tribes reassert themselves.

406

★ EVENTS   Roman military occupation of Britain draws to a close
as Constantine III withdraws forces to support his claim to
the imperial title.

409

★ EVENTS   (c.) In light of the Roman evacuation, the Saxons
renew their invasion efforts.

The British rebel against continued government from Rome by
Constantine III and throw off Roman rule once and for all.

418

★ EVENTS   With Rome itself under serious threat from the
Goths, the Romans in Britain gather all their hordes of gold
and either bury it or transport it to Gaul. Anxiety about the
safety of Rome results in further diminution of Roman
authority in Britain.

430

⭐ EVENTS   Pope Celestine I sends the Roman author Palladius
as his envoy to preach Christianity to the Scots.

446

⭐ EVENTS   The Saxon onslaught against Britain continues. The
Britons appeal first to the Romans, then to the Angles for
aid.

448

⭐ EVENTS   Vortigern, King of the Britons, receives the Angles
under Hengist and Horsa to help defend the country.

455

⭐ EVENTS   The Angles turn against the Britons. Horsa is killed
in the course of the action.

456

⭐ EVENTS   Hengist decisively defeats the Britons and puts them
to flight.

477

⭐ EVENTS   The Britons come under constant military
subjugation by the Saxons (until the end of the century).

6th Century

500

⭐ EVENTS   (c.) Angles and Saxons set up permanent habitation
in Britain.

(c.) Kingdom of Wessex is established (to c.550).

515

⭐ EVENTS   The Britons achieve a decisive victory at the Battle
of Mount Badon, halting the West Saxon advance.

519

★ EVENTS   Cerdic, Saxon leader and ancestor of Alfred, the Great, takes control of the future kingdom of Wessex and becomes king of the West Saxons.

521

★ EVENTS   St Columba, Irish apostle of Christianity in Scotland, is born.

525

★ EVENTS   (c.) Bernicia, coastal territory around Banburgh, established by the Angles (to 550).

534

★ EVENTS   Cerdic, king of the West Saxons, dies and is succeeded by his son (or possibly grandson) Cynric.

547

★ EVENTS   Banburgh is built as a defensive settlement by King Ida of Bernicia.

560

★ EVENTS   Cynric, King of the West Saxons, dies and is succeeded by Ceawlin, his son. Having driven the Britons from Wessex, Ceawlin becomes second overlord of the southern English.

563

★ EVENTS   St Columba founds the monastery on Iona that becomes the mother church of Celtic Christianity in Scotland.

Exploration of the North Atlantic, Northern Isles, Faroes and Iceland from bases in Northern Scotland (to 583).

574

★ EVENTS   Aiden is anointed as King of Dal Riada (effectively King of Scots) by Columba.

577

☆ EVENTS Following the defeat of the Britons at the Battle of Dyrham, the Saxons again begin to expand.

584

☆ EVENTS Founding of the Anglo-Saxon kingdom of Mercia. Birth of Edwin, later king of Northumbria.

585

☆ EVENTS (c.) Durrow founded by Columba (to 589).

590

☆ EVENTS (c.) Gregory I (the Great), one of the Church fathers, becomes pope.

591

☆ EVENTS Ceawlin, King of Wessex, is defeated in battle at Adam's Grave and succeeded by Ceol. Hussa, King of Bernicia, is succeeded after his death by Ethelfrith.

597

✝ DEATHS Columba: Irish apostle of Christianity in Scotland. Dies on Iona; pilgrims begin arriving immediately.

☆ EVENTS (c.) Augustine, sent by Pope Gregory I to Britain, brings Christianity to the Anglo-Saxons.

7th century

600

☆ EVENTS (c.) Slaughter of northern Britons during failed attack on Angles at Catterick.

604

✝ DEATHS St Augustine (birth date unknown): Italian churchman and Archbishop of Canterbury, sent to convert the Anglo-Saxons to Christianity.

☆ EVENTS   Before his death, Augustine appoints two bishops to
preach Christianity to the East Saxons.

Numerous Britons, including 200 priests, slaughtered by
Ethelfrith, King of Northumbria, at Chester.

607

☆ EVENTS   (c.) Ethelfrith defeats the Welsh, again at Chester.

616

☆ EVENTS   Edwin succeeds as King of Northumbria and
becomes fifth overlord of the English following the death of
his father, Ethelfrith.

620

☆ EVENTS   Ireland invaded by Norsemen.

624/625

☆ EVENTS   Raedwald, King of East Anglia, dies and is buried at
Sutton Hoo. It is probably his ship burial that is uncovered in
1939.

626

☆ EVENTS   Edinburgh founded by Edwin of Northumbria.

627

☆ EVENTS   Paulinus, Roman Christian missionary, takes mission
to the Angles in Northumbria.

Edwin, King of Northumbria, is baptized by Paulinus. This
follows the apparent empowering of Edwin by Paulinus
through prayer to overthrow an enemy who has tried to
assassinate him.

632

☆ EVENTS   Northumbrian army defeated at Hatfield by
combined Welsh and Mercian force.

633

✝ DEATHS Edwin: King of Northumbria.

634

✿ BIRTHS St Wilfrid: English prelate.

635

✿ BIRTHS (c.) St Cuthbert: Anglo-Saxon churchman and missionary.

636

✭ EVENTS Foundation of the religious community at Lindisfarne by Bishop Aiden.

638

✭ EVENTS Edinburgh attacked by Northumbrians, while Anglian conquests threaten the Forth.

650

✭ EVENTS (c.) The earliest known example of Celtic Christian art, *The Book of Durrow*, is completed.

651

✭ EVENTS (c.) Cuthbert, Anglo-Saxon churchman and missionary, enters the monastery at Melrose after seeing a divine vision at the time of the death of Bishop Aiden.

654

✭ EVENTS Mercians defeated by Northumbrians at Battle of Winwaed.

655

✭ EVENTS (c.) Wilfred is made Bishop of York and becomes involved in controversy over the organization of the church in Britain.

660

★ EVENTS   Foundation of the Augustinian monastery at Canterbury.

663

★ EVENTS   Outbreak of plague hits Britain.

664

★ EVENTS   Cuthbert becomes prior of Lindisfarne.

Roman Catholicism adopted by the Synod of Whitby.

670

★ EVENTS   Northumbrian ascendancy over Britain ends with the death of King Oswui, succeeded by Egfrith.

672

❀ BIRTHS   (c.) St Boniface (originally, Wynfrith): English Benedictine missionary, known as the 'Apostle of Germany'.

First synod of the English church at Hertford.

673

❀ BIRTHS   Bede: Anglo-Saxon scholar, historian and theologian.

North-western Scottish Picts evangelized.

Cuthbert becomes bishop of Lindisfarne.

674

★ EVENTS   For the first time, English churches have glass windows.

678

★ EVENTS   (c.) Wilfred, Bishop of York, appeals to Rome to settle the issue of the division of Northumbria into four sees (areas under the religious authority of bishops or archbishops).

A comet appears and endures for three months.

682

✯ EVENTS   Bede leaves the Benedictine monastery at
Wearmouth and moves to the new monastery at Jarrow, where
he is ordained, and where he will remain for the rest of his
life. His greatest work will be the *Historia Ecclesiatica Gentis
Anglorum* (Ecclesiastical History of the English People), the
source of almost all information on the history of England
before 731, said to have been translated into English by Alfred,
the Great.

685

✯ EVENTS   Northumbrian domination of England is finally
thwarted after the Battle of Nectansmere. Pictish victory
prevents Northumbrians overrunning Scotland.

Ceadwalla becomes King of Wessex following the overthrow of
Centwine.

686

✯ EVENTS   Sussex, Britain's last non-Christian kingdom, is
converted.

687

✝ DEATHS   St Cuthbert: Anglo-Saxon churchman and
missionary.

✯ EVENTS   Ceadwalla, King of Wessex, attacks Kent.

688

✯ EVENTS   Ceadwalla departs for Rome leaving the throne of
Wessex for Ine, who establishes himself and his issue as kings
of the West Saxons and draws up a set of laws which are the
oldest to survive in Britain.

690

✯ EVENTS   The last Roman archbishop, Theodorus, dies.

692

✯ EVENTS   Brihtwold becomes the first English Archbishop of
Canterbury.

698

⭐ EVENTS   (c.) *The Lindisfarne Gospels* are written and
illuminated.

8th Century

700

⭐ EVENTS   (c.) The Psalms are translated into Anglo-Saxon.

712

⭐ EVENTS   (c.) Columban clergy in Iona persuaded to accept
Roman usage.

715

⭐ EVENTS   Battle at Adam's Grave between Ine of Wessex and
Ceolred of Mercia.

718

⭐ EVENTS   St Boniface (Wynfrith) is commissioned to preach
the gospel to all the tribes of Germany, meets with great
success, and is made Bishop, Primate of Germany (732) and
Archbishop of Mainz (746).

725

⭐ EVENTS   (c.) It is reported that Irish monks from the Scottish
Northern Isles are now travelling to the Faroes.

King Wihtred of Kent dies after a 34 year reign and is succeeded
by his son Ethelbert II.

731

⭐ EVENTS   *Ecclesiastical History of the English People* completed
by Bede.

735

✝ DEATHS   Bede: Anglo-Saxon scholar, historian and
theologian. Heralds the end of a great period of
Northumbrian scholarship.

741

✵ EVENTS   The burning of York.

754

✝ DEATHS   St Boniface (originally, Wynfrith): English
Benedictine missionary, known as the 'Apostle of Germany'.
Killed by the heathen in Frisia.

756

✵ EVENTS   The burning of Canterbury.

760

✵ EVENTS   (c.) Completion of the *Book of Kells*, Latin gospels
written in Irish in an elaborate illuminated form.

757

✵ EVENTS   Mercian civil war.

Offa takes control of Mercia, thus uniting much of England
under his rule.

774

✵ EVENTS   Northumbrian rebellion against their king, Alhred,
results in his deposition and the crowning of Ethelred I.

776

✵ EVENTS   Battle between Mercian and Kentish armies at Otford
in Kent.

779

✵ EVENTS   Offa, King of Mercia, becomes the first King of all
England.

787

✵ EVENTS   Early Viking raids.

793

✵ EVENTS   (c.) St Albans Abbey founded as a monastery by
Offa.

Vikings sack Lindisfarne and Jarrow.

Offa annexes East Anglia and joins it to the kingdom of Mercia.

795

★ EVENTS   Vikings raid Iona and Ireland.

796

★ EVENTS   Death of Offa, King of Mercia (birth date unknown).
The greatest Anglo-Saxon ruler of the 8th century. Styling
himself 'King of the English', he asserted his authority over
all the kingdoms south of the Humber. He was responsible
for constructing Offa's Dyke, and establishing a new currency
based on the silver penny. His reign represents an important
but flawed attempt to unify England, with Mercian supremacy
collapsing soon after his death.

9th Century

800

★ EVENTS   (c.) Iona hit by three Viking attacks around this time.

810

★ EVENTS   *Historia Britonum* (History of Britain) written by the
Welsh monk Nynniaw.

815

★ EVENTS   Egbert, King of Wessex, attacks Cornwall.

821

✝ DEATHS   King Cenwulf of Mercia: his death brings Mercian
domination of England to an end.

825

✝ DEATHS   Beornwulf, King of the Mercians, killed by the East
Angles.

★ EVENTS   Egbert, King of Wessex, is victorious over the
Mercians at Ellendun (now Wroughton) in Wiltshire; Essex,
Kent, Surrey, and Sussex all submit to him.

Vikings raid the church on Iona, killing the bishop and setting the building on fire.

Egbert of Wessex deposes Baldred of Kent allowing Kent, Sussex and Essex to be united under one West Saxon king.

827

✪ EVENTS   Following his conquest of Mercia, Egbert of Wessex controls all of England south of the Humber.

Egbert then turns on Northumbria which submits to his dominance.

828

✪ EVENTS   Egbert of Wessex recognized as overlord of the 'Seven Kingdoms of the Heptarchy'.

829

✪ EVENTS   The earlier conquest of Mercia by Egbert of Wessex is reversed.

830

✿ BIRTHS   (c.) Ethelred I: King of Wessex, the elder brother of Alfred, the Great.

835

✪ EVENTS   Kent coast becomes target for Danish raids.

836

✪ EVENTS   Egbert of Wessex is defeated by invasion force of Danes.

838

✪ EVENTS   Egbert of Wessex extends his control over Cornwall, defeating an alliance between the Vikings and Britons at Hingston Down. These successes give him mastery over southern England from Kent to Land's End, and establish Wessex as the strongest Anglo-Saxon kingdom.

839

✝ DEATHS   Egbert: King of Wessex. He is succeeded by his two
sons; Ethelwulf as King of Wessex, and Athelstan as king of
Kent, Essex, Sussex and Surrey.

King of the Picts, killed by the Danes.

840

★ EVENTS   Vikings land and winter on British coasts.

(c.) The Stone of Destiny (a revered sandstone relic on which
successive monarchs are crowned) is removed probably from
Iona to Scone Abbey by King Kenelm II.

841

★ EVENTS   Vikings savagely raid Kent, East Anglia and
Lincolnshire, killing many.

Dublin and Limerick founded by the Vikings, with Dublin
becoming the main Viking base in Ireland.

842

★ EVENTS   Many die in London and Rochester during Viking
raids.

844

★ EVENTS   The Kingdom of Alba is formed when Kenneth I
(MacAlpin) becomes King of the Scots and Picts.

845

★ EVENTS   Danes are defeated by a Saxon force at the River
Parrett.

849

✾ BIRTHS   Alfred, the Great: King of Wessex, son of King
Ethelwulf.

851

★ EVENTS   London is invaded by a massive Viking force which
then proceeds into Surrey via Canterbury, sacking the
cathedral: it is eventually stopped by a Saxon army.

855

✴ EVENTS Alfred, the Great, goes on a pilgrimage to Rome with his father, Ethelwulf of Wessex, and stays for a year.

858

♱ DEATHS Kenneth I (MacAlpin) (birth date unknown): King of the Scots and Picts. He combined the territories of both peoples in a united kingdom of Scotia (Scotland north of the Forth–Clyde line), and also moved the centre of the Church from Iona to Dunkeld.

865

✴ EVENTS A truce is agreed between the Danes and the people of Kent, but is broken by the Danes, who continue to carry out raids.

866

✴ EVENTS (c.) Danes establish North British kingdom.

870

❀ BIRTHS (c.) Edward the Elder: King of Wessex, son of Alfred, the Great. He will build on his father's successes and establish himself as the strongest ruler in Britain.

✴ EVENTS East Anglia bears the brunt of a savage attack by the main Viking army. Edmund, King of East Anglia, is killed when he refuses to submit to Danish rule.

871

♱ DEATHS Ethelred I: King of Wessex, the elder brother of Alfred, the Great. It was during Ethelred's reign that the Danes launched their main invasion of England. He dies soon after his victory over the invaders.

✴ EVENTS Guthrum, Danish king of East Anglia, leads a major Viking invasion of Anglo-Saxon England (the 'Great Summer Army'), seizes East Anglia and conquers Northumbria and Mercia.

Alfred, the Great, becomes King of Wessex following the death of his brother Ethelred I.

872

★ EVENTS   London falls to the Viking invaders.

875

★ EVENTS   After persistent attacks by the Vikings, the monks of
Lindisfarne take to travelling through Northumbria and
Galloway with the *Lindisfarne Gospels* and the relics of St
Aiden, St Oswald and St Cuthbert. It is eight years before
they return to the Holy Isle.

Creation of the Viking kingdom of York.

876

★ EVENTS   Collapse of the Kingdom of Northumbria.

878

★ EVENTS   Guthrum, Danish king of East Anglia, attacks Wessex
and drives Alfred, the Great, into hiding in Somerset.

Alfred, the Great, inflicts on the Danes their first major reversal
at the Battle of Edington in Wiltshire. In the ensuing treaty,
Guthrum agrees to leave Wessex and accept baptism as a
Christian, and he and his army settle down peacefully in East
Anglia. The West Saxons are established as England's
dominant power.

879

★ EVENTS   Treaty of Wedmore: between Alfred, the Great, and
the Viking leader Guthrum. In return for his submission to
baptism, Guthrum is ceded territory in England.

885

★ EVENTS   Alfred, the Great, King of the West Saxons, imposes
his rule over south Wales.

886

★ EVENTS   Alfred, the Great, begins to win back Danish-
occupied territory by capturing the former Mercian town of
London.

The Danelaw — the territory occupied by the Danes in East Anglia — is formally recognized by Alfred.

890

✝ DEATHS Guthrum (birth date unknown): Danish King of East Anglia and opponent of King Alfred, the Great.

✴ EVENTS (c.) Alfred, the Great, as part of his extension of the power of the King's court, introduces a permanent regular militia and navy.

891

✴ EVENTS (c.) Circulation of the manuscripts of the *Anglo-Saxon Chronicle*, a primary source of information on early British history. It recounts chronologically events in Anglo-Saxon and Norman Britain.

892

✴ EVENTS A sizeable Viking force invades England, but has little success.

893

✴ EVENTS (c.) Asser, Bishop of Sherborne, completes his *Life of Alfred, the Great*.

895

✿ BIRTHS Athelstan: King of England, son of Edward the Elder, and grandson of Alfred, the Great.

899

✝ DEATHS Alfred, the Great: King of Wessex, son of King Ethelwulf. He stole the military initiative from the Danes by reorganizing his forces into a standing army, building a navy, and establishing a network of burhs (fortified centres). He also revived religion and learning, forged close ties with other English peoples not under Danish rule, and provided his successors with the means to reconquer the Danelaw and secure the unity of England.

10th Century

901

★ EVENTS   Edward the Elder proclaims himself 'King of the
  Angles and Saxons'.

909

❀ BIRTHS   (c.) Dunstan: Anglo-Saxon prelate. Founder of the
  Benedictine rule in England.

910

★ EVENTS   In one of the most decisive military campaigns (to
  918) of the whole Anglo-Saxon period, Edward the Elder
  conquers and annexes to Wessex the southern Danelaw.

918

★ EVENTS   Edward the Elder assumes control of southern
  England and is accepted as overlord by the kings of Wales.

919

★ EVENTS   Edward the Elder is accepted as overlord by Ragnald,
  ruler of the Viking Kingdom of York.

920

★ EVENTS   Although he exercises no direct power in the north,
  all the chief rulers beyond the Humber, including the King
  of Scots, formally recognize the overlordship of Edward the
  Elder.

921

❀ BIRTHS   Edmund I: King of the English, half-brother of
  Athelstan.

924

✝ DEATHS   Edward the Elder: King of Wessex, son of Alfred, the
  Great.

⭐ **EVENTS**   Athelstan becomes King of Wessex and Mercia on the death of his father Edward the Elder.

926

✿ **BIRTHS**   (c.) Brian: King of Ireland, also known as 'Brian Boru' (Brian of the tribute).

⭐ **EVENTS**   Edward the Elder's successor Athelstan renews the oaths of allegiance made to his father by the Welsh, Scots and Danish kings.

927

⭐ **EVENTS**   Athelstan invades Northumbria, securing his direct rule over it, and thus establishing himself as effectively the first King of all England.

937

⭐ **EVENTS**   Athelstan stabilizes his position as King of all England by defeating a powerful coalition of Scots, Welsh and Danes at Brunanburh (location unknown).

939

✝ **DEATHS**   Athelstan: King of England, son of Edward the Elder, and grandson of Alfred, the Great.

⭐ **EVENTS**   On Edmund I's accession to the English throne, Scandinavian forces from Northumbria, with reinforcements from Ireland, overrun the East Midlands.

942

⭐ **EVENTS**   Edmund I re-establishes his control over the south Danelaw.

943

✿ **BIRTHS**   Edgar: King of Mercia, Northumbria and all England, son of Edmund I.

944

⭐ **EVENTS**   Edmund re-establishes his control over Northumbria and rules a united England.

945

★ EVENTS The Scots under Malcolm I annexe Westmoreland and Cumberland.

Dunstan is appointed abbot at Glastonbury abbey; he transforms it into a centre of religious teaching.

946

✝ DEATHS Edmund I: King of the English, half-brother of Athelstan.

947

★ EVENTS York is again subjugated to Danish control under Erik Blood-axe, who loses it the next year.

954

✝ DEATHS Erik Blood-axe, last Danish king of York, is killed when he and his followers are driven from York. This results in the permanent unification of England.

959

★ EVENTS Edgar, King of Mercia and Northumberland, becomes King of all England.

962

❀ BIRTHS (c.) Edward the Martyr: King of England, son of Edgar. During his reign there will be a reaction against the policies in support of monasticism that had been espoused by his father.

963

★ EVENTS First record of the existence of London Bridge.

964

★ EVENTS Following the devastation inflicted upon the monasteries of Britain by the Vikings, a monastic revival begins.

965

✴ EVENTS   Westminster Abbey is founded.

968

❀ BIRTHS   (c.) Ethelred the Unready: King of England, son of
Edgar, aged about 10 when the murder of his half-brother,
Edward the Martyr, will place him on the throne.

973

✴ EVENTS   Edgar is recognized as Emperor of England at a
coronation ceremony near Bath.

(c.) Edgar of England introduces a uniform currency based on
silver pennies.

974

✴ EVENTS   Occurrence of the first verified earthquake in Britain.

975

✟ DEATHS   Edgar: King of Mercia, Northumbria and all
England, son of Edmund I. He encouraged the reform of the
English Church as a means of enhancing his prestige and
power, though his lavish support for the monasteries caused
bitterness among the nobility.

✴ EVENTS   (c.) Copying of the *Exeter Book*, the largest existing
volume of English poetry.

976

✴ EVENTS   Brian Boru becomes chief of Dál Cais.

978

✟ DEATHS   Edward the Martyr: King of England, son of Edgar.
He is murdered at Corfe, Dorset, by supporters of his
stepmother, Elfrida.

Ethelred the Unready, son of Edgar, becomes young King of
England after the murder of his half-brother Edward the
Martyr.

980

❀ BIRTHS (c.) Edmund II, 'Ironside': King of the English, son of Ethelred the Unready.

★ EVENTS (c.) Renewed attacks by the Vikings on England begin as raids throughout the 980s.

984

★ EVENTS Brian Boru makes himself King of Leinster and further campaigns lead to his rule being acknowledged over all Ireland.

985

★ EVENTS Sweyn I, Forkbeard, rebels against his father, Harold Blue-tooth, and deposes him.

986

★ EVENTS Iona is again victim of Viking raids.

988

✝ DEATHS Dunstan: Anglo-Saxon prelate. Founder of the Benedictine rule in England.

991

★ EVENTS Battle of Maldon: Danes achieve their first victory over the English for 100 years.

First levy of the Danegeld, a tax raised to buy peace from the Viking invaders (to 1016). In this year alone, 10,000 pounds of silver are paid. After 1066, the term is used for the general geld (tax) which is effectively abolished in 1162.

994

★ EVENTS Beginning of a series of military campaigns against England by Sweyn I, Forkbeard. On each occasion, King Ethelred the Unready pays escalating amounts of Danegeld to buy off the Danish invaders but they continue to return for more.

995

⚘ BIRTHS   (c.) Canute (Cnut): King of England, Denmark and
      Norway, son of Sweyn I, Forkbeard. He will rule England
      according to the accepted traditions of English kingship, and
      maintain the peace throughout his reign.

★ EVENTS   The wandering Lindisfarne community resettles in
      Durham.

11th Century

The 11th century was a period of significant change in the culture
of the British Isles, and of England particularly, due to the Norman
Conquest and the resultant influence of Norman culture on the
English court and nobility which followed it.

The century witnessed a flurry of architectural activity, especially in
church building. Exeter and Winchester Cathedrals, Battle Abbey,
Westminster Abbey and York Cathedral were all built in this century
along with Richmond and Carlisle Castles and the Tower of London.
From 1066, British architecture was in the Norman, or Romanesque
style. In church architecture this included the appearance of towers
and the beginning of the common inclusion of aisles and transepts
(which roughly formed cross-shaped floor plans). Timber remained
the usual material for church construction until the 12th century.

The Norman invasion also led to the creation of the most notable
work of art to come out of Britain in the 11th century: the Bayeux
Tapestry. This 68m-long embroidered wall hanging shows the events
leading up to the Norman Conquest, including the Battle of
Hastings, and provides much detail of clothing and lifestyle in
England at this time.

An important work of literature dating from this period is the
Mabinogion, a collection of tales written in Welsh which incorporate
some aspects of French Arthurian legend and also show other
European influences.

1001

✸ EVENTS   Canonization of Edward the Martyr.

1002

✸ EVENTS   Ethelred the Unready confirms an alliance with
Normandy by marrying, as his second wife, Duke Richard's
daughter Emma — the first dynastic link between the two
countries.

1003

✿ BIRTHS   (c.) Edward the Confessor: King of England, son of
Ethelred the Unready and last king in the Old English royal
line.

1005

✿ BIRTHS   (c.) Macbeth: King of Scots, probably a grandson of
Kenneth II, son of Findleach, Mormaer of Moray, and
nephew of Malcolm II. In contrast with his later malign
Shakespearean image, he will rule wisely, avoiding expensive
and debilitating raids on England.

1010

✿ BIRTHS   (c.) Duncan I: King of Scots, the grandson of
Malcolm II.

1013

✸ EVENTS   Sweyn I, Forkbeard, invades England with his son
Canute, and secures mastery over the whole country, forcing
Ethelred the Unready into exile in Normandy.

1014

✝ DEATHS   Sweyn I, Forkbeard, (birth date unknown): King of
Denmark and, for five weeks before his death, of England.

Brian: King of Ireland, also known as 'Brian Boru' (Brian of the
tribute). He is killed after defeating the Vikings at Clontarf.

✸ EVENTS   After death of Sweyn I, Forkbeard, Ethelred the
Unready returns from exile to oppose Canute, but the unity

of English resistance is broken when his son, Edmund II, 'Ironside', rebels.

1016

✿ BIRTHS (c.) Harold I, Harefoot: King of England, son of Canute.

✟ DEATHS Ethelred the Unready: King of England, son of Edgar.

Edmund II, 'Ironside': son of Ethelred the Unready.

✯ EVENTS Edmund II is chosen to be King of England by the Londoners on his father's death, while Canute is elected at Southampton by the Witan (Anglo-Saxon council). Edmund hastily levies an army, defeats Canute, and attempts to raise the siege of London, but is routed at Ashingdon, or possibly Ashdon, Essex. He agrees to a partition of the country, but dies a few weeks later, leaving Canute as sole ruler of all England.

1018

✿ BIRTHS Hardicanute: King of Denmark and of England, son of Canute.

1022

✿ BIRTHS Harold II: last Anglo-Saxon King of England, son of Earl Godwin, nominated for the monarchy by Edward the Confessor.

1028

✿ BIRTHS (c.) William I, 'the Conqueror': Duke of Normandy and the first Norman King of England, illegitimate son of Duke Robert of Normandy.

1031

✿ BIRTHS (c.) Malcolm III, 'Canmore' ('large-headed'): King of Scots, son of Duncan I.

1033

✿ BIRTHS   (c.) Donald III ('Donald Bane'): King of Scots, son
of Duncan I. His reign will be brief and turbulent.

1035

✝ DEATHS   Canute (Cnut): King of England, Denmark and
Norway, son of Sweyn I, Forkbeard. He ruled England,
according to the accepted traditions of English kingship, and
maintained the peace throughout his reign.

1037

✪ EVENTS   Following death of Canute, his son Hardicanute is
heir, but is unable to come to England immediately to claim
the throne. The English elect his half-brother, Harold I,
Harefoot, regent in his stead, and then confirm Harold as
King.

1040

✝ DEATHS   (c.) Duncan I: King of Scots, grandson of Malcolm
II. He succeeded to Strathclyde and probably ruled over most
of Scotland except the islands and the far north. He attempted
southwards expansion and a long and unsuccessful siege of
Durham weakened his position. He is killed by Macbeth at
Pitgaveney, near Elgin, and Macbeth assumes the Scottish
throne.

Harold I, Harefoot: King of England, son of Canute.

✪ EVENTS   Hardicanute mounts an expedition to invade
England to claim the crown, but Harold dies before he arrives.
Hardicanute is thereupon elected King, and promptly
punishes the English by imposing a savage fleet-tax to pay for
his expedition.

1042

✝ DEATHS   Hardicanute: King of Denmark and of England, son
of Canute. Dies of convulsions at a drinking party.

1045

❀ BIRTHS   (c.) Margaret: Scottish queen, wife of Malcolm III, 'Canmore', King of Scotland. She will do much to civilize the realm, and assimilate the old Celtic Church to the rest of Christendom.

✯ EVENTS   Macbeth defeats a challenge to his kingship from Crinan, father of Duncan I.

1054

✯ EVENTS   Malcolm III, 'Canmore', of Scotland returns from exile and conquers southern Scotland.

1056

❀ BIRTHS   (c.) William II, 'Rufus': King of England, son of William I, the Conqueror.

1057

✝ DEATHS   Macbeth: King of Scots. He is defeated and killed by Malcolm III, 'Canmore', son of Duncan I, at Lumphanan on 15 Aug, after an invasion from England aided by Earl Siward of Northumbria.

1058

✯ EVENTS   Malcolm III, 'Canmore' becomes king of Scotland after his defeat and killing of Macbeth (1057), and disposal of Macbeth's stepson, Lulach (1058).

1060

❀ BIRTHS   (c.) Duncan II: King of Scots, son of Malcolm III, 'Canmore'.

1066

✝ DEATHS   Edward the Confessor: King of England, son of Ethelred the Unready and last king in the Old English royal line. Edward was childless, and on his deathbed in London apparently nominated Harold Godwin (Harold II) to succeed him. However, some controversy surrounds this as William I also claimed to have been nominated by him.

⭐ EVENTS   Harold III, Hardrada, invades England to claim the
  throne after the death of Edward the Confessor, but is
  defeated and killed by Harold II at Stamford Bridge.

William I invades England. Apparently nominated by Edward
  the Confessor as future King of England (1051), he invades
  with the support of the papacy when Harold Godwin takes
  the throne as Harold II.

(14 Oct) Battle of Hastings: William I, 'the Conqueror', defeats
  Harold II, who is shot through the eye with an arrow and
  killed.

William I is crowned King, beginning the rule of a dynasty of
  Norman kings (1066–1154), and entailing the virtual
  replacement of the Anglo-Saxon nobility with Normans,
  Bretons, and Flemings, many of whom retain lands in
  northern France. Between 1066 and 1144 England and
  Normandy are normally united under one king-duke, and
  the result is the formation of a single cross-Channel state.

Establishment of the Curia Regis: the king's household and a
  fluctuating entourage of important subjects, which conduct
  all the central functions of government in early medieval times.

1067

⭐ EVENTS   (c.) Creation of the Bayeux Tapestry (to c.1077): an
  embroidered wall-hanging in coloured wool on linen, which
  narrates events leading up to the invasion of England by
  William of Normandy ('the Conqueror'), and the Battle of
  Hastings in 1066. It is probably commissioned by William's
  half-brother Odo, Bishop of Bayeux in northern France, and
  embroidered in southern England.

1068

❀ BIRTHS   Henry I: King of England and Duke of Normandy,
  son of William I, 'the Conqueror'.

1077

❀ BIRTHS   (c.) Alexander I: King of Scotland, son of Malcolm
  III, 'Canmore'.

1080

✿ BIRTHS   (c.) David I: King of Scotland, son of Malcolm III, 'Canmore' and Margaret.

✟ DEATHS   Lady Godiva (birth date unknown): English noblewoman and religious benefactress. According to tradition, she rode naked through Coventry marketplace in order to persuade her husband Leofric to reduce a heavy tax imposed upon the townsfolk (1040).

1086

★ EVENTS   Domesday Book: the great survey of England south of the Ribble and Tees Rivers (London and Winchester excepted), compiled on the orders of William I. Information is arranged by county and, within each county, according to tenure by major landholders; each manor is described according to value and resources. Domesday was one of the greatest administrative achievements of the Middle Ages, yet its central purpose remains unclear. Most probably, it was to assist the royal exploitation of crown lands and feudal rights, and to provide the new nobility with a formal record and confirmation of their lands, thus putting a final seal on the Norman occupation.

1087

✟ DEATHS   William I, 'the Conqueror': Duke of Normandy and the first Norman King of England, illegitimate son of Duke Robert of Normandy. Dies while defending Normandy's southern border.

1090

✿ BIRTHS   (c.) Stephen: last Norman king of England, son of Stephen, Count of Blois.

     (c.) William of Malmesbury: English chronicler and Benedictine monk.

1093

✟ DEATHS   Malcolm III, 'Canmore': King of Scots, son of Duncan I. Killed in battle against the English at Alnwick.

Margaret: Scottish queen, wife of Malcolm III, 'Canmore', King of Scotland.

✭ EVENTS   After the death of Malcolm III, 'Canmore', William II, 'Rufus', exercises a controlling influence over Scottish affairs.

1094

✝ DEATHS   Duncan II: King of Scots, son of Malcolm III. Killed, probably at the instigation of Donald III.

1096

✭ EVENTS   First Crusade (to 1099).

Robert Curthose relinquishes the struggle against his brother William II of England for control of Normandy and departs on the First Crusade. William rules the duchy as de facto duke.

1097

✭ EVENTS   Donald III of Scotland overthrown by an English army in support of the claim of Edgar, Malcolm III's eldest surviving son by his marriage to Margaret.

12th Century

Britain in the 12th century was not yet one country, but its component parts (England, Scotland, Ireland and Wales) were sufficiently linked to allow them to influence each other culturally as well as make war on each other. France was also greatly influential on British culture in the early Middle Ages due to the Norman Conquest and the large number of French nobles brought to the court of England by William the Conqueror.

Art and architecture in the 1100s were especially influenced by continental developments. In addition, crusaders returning from the Holy Lands brought back Eastern (Byzantine) influences. The production of illuminated manuscripts increased as new religious orders and monasteries were founded. The use of elaborate initials on these manuscripts was accompanied by a variety of depictions of events, monsters and people which became increasingly sophisticated as the century progressed, until eventually this Romanesque illumination became Gothic. In architecture, the 12th century experienced this transition also, with the lapsing of the Romanesque (two tower façade and early ribbed vaults) and the development of the early Gothic (pointed arches and more sophisticated ribbed vaults).

In English literature, Middle English gradually superseded Old English as the preferred language. Also greatly important was the introduction into English of the Arthurian legend by Geoffrey of Monmouth in his *Historia Regum Britanniae*. The influence of continental literature was marked by the increasing incidence of the courtly love tradition in English writing — a form already popular in France and Germany, which revolved around the love (usually unfulfilled) of a knight for a lady, with definite religious undertones.

1100

✿ BIRTHS (c.) Adrian IV (Nicholas Breakspear): English Pope
(1154–9), the only Englishman to hold the office.

Geoffrey of Monmouth: Welsh chronicler, consecrated Bishop
of St Asaph in 1152.

✝ DEATHS William II, 'Rufus': King of England, son of William
I, the Conqueror. Killed by an arrow while hunting in the
New Forest.

(c.) Donald III ('Donald Bane'): King of Scots, son of Duncan
I. Blinded and killed by his rival, Edgar.

1102

✺ EVENTS Henry I of England has the tomb of Edward the
Confessor opened to discover that the body has not decayed.

1106

✺ EVENTS Battle of Tinchebrai: Henry I of England conquers
Normandy after defeating his brother, Duke of Normandy.

1109

✺ EVENTS War between England and France (to 1113).

1118

✿ BIRTHS Thomas à Becket: English saint, martyr and
Archbishop of Canterbury.

✺ EVENTS England is governed by a vice-regal committee while
Henry I is at war in France.

1119

✺ EVENTS Foundation of the Order of the Knights Templar:
religious military order established to protect pilgrims
travelling to Jerusalem during the Crusades.

1124

✝ DEATHS Alexander I: King of Scotland, son of Malcolm III,
'Canmore'.

1128

★ EVENTS   Matilda, Henry I's only surviving legitimate child, is married to Geoffrey Plantagenet. Henry's barons are forced to swear that they will make her Queen on his death.

1133

❀ BIRTHS   Henry II (Henry of Anjou): King of England. Son of Henry, Count of Anjou.

1135

✝ DEATHS   Henry I: King of England and Duke of Normandy, son of William I, the Conqueror. During his reign, the Norman empire attained the height of its power as he conquered Normandy, maintained his position on the Continent, and exercised varying degrees of authority over the King of Scots, the Welsh princes, the Duke of Brittany, and also the Counts of Flanders, Boulogne, and Ponthieu. His government of England and Normandy had become increasingly centralized and interventionist, with the overriding aim of financing warfare and alliances, and consolidating the unity of the two countries as a single cross-Channel state.

★ EVENTS   Stephen of Blois seizes English crown on death of Henry I; civil war breaks out between supporters of Stephen and those of Matilda.

1136

★ EVENTS   As a nominal supporter of the claims of his niece, Matilda, to the English crown, David I of Scotland embarks on wars of territorial conquest against Stephen of England.

1137

★ EVENTS   Adrian IV appointed abbot of the monastery of St Rufus, near Avignon.

1138

★ EVENTS   Battle of the Standard: defeat of David I of Scotland, fighting on behalf of Matilda in English civil war.

1139

★ EVENTS   Matilda lands in England, supported by her half-brother, the Earl of Gloucester.

Outbreak of anti-semitism in England and France following the murder of a young boy, later St William of Norwich, believed sacrificed by the Jews.

1140

❀ BIRTHS   Hubert Walter: English churchman, statesman and Bishop of Salisbury.

1141

❀ BIRTHS   (c.) Malcolm IV, 'the maiden': King of Scotland, grandson of David I. His name arises from his reputation for chastity.

★ EVENTS   (Feb) Battle of Lincoln: Matilda captures Stephen of England and rules as Queen. Stephen restored after popular rising.

David I of Scotland occupies the whole of northern England to the Ribble and the Tees.

1142

❀ BIRTHS   (c.) William I, 'the Lion': King of Scots, brother and successor of Malcolm IV. Despite his difficulties with England, he will make Scotland a much stronger kingdom.

1143

✝ DEATHS   (c.) William of Malmesbury: English chronicler and Benedictine monk, he emphasized the importance of documentary material and non-written sources (eg architectural evidence). His main works were *Gesta Regum Anglorum*, a general history of England from the coming of the Anglo-Saxons; *Gesta Pontificum Anglorum*, an ecclesiastical history of England from the Conversion; and *Historia Novella*, a contemporary narrative of English affairs from c.1125 to 1142.

1146

✯ EVENTS   Adrian IV appointed Cardinal Bishop of Albano by
Pope Eugenius III, after an attempt to defame his character
fails.

1147

✯ EVENTS   Following the death of her main supporter, Robert
of Gloucester, Matilda's campaign for the throne loses
impetus.

Second Crusade (to 1149).

1148

✯ EVENTS   Matilda abandons her struggle to be recognized as
Queen and leaves England permanently.

1150

❀ BIRTHS   (c.) Stephen Langton: English prelate and Archbishop
of Canterbury. Pope Innocent III will make him a cardinal
(1206) and Archbishop (1207), but King John will refuse to
accept his appointment, and Langton will be kept out of the
see (the area under religious authority) until 1213.

1153

✟ DEATHS   David I: King of Scotland, son of Malcolm III,
'Canmore', and (St) Margaret.

✯ EVENTS   Henry of Anjou invades England and forces Stephen
to make him heir to the English throne.

1154

✟ DEATHS   Stephen: last Norman king of England, son of
Stephen, Count of Blois.

Geoffrey of Monmouth: Welsh chronicler, consecrated Bishop
of St Asaph in 1152. His *Historia Regum Britanniae* (History
of the Kings of Britain), composed before 1147, introduced
the stories of King Lear and Cymbeline, the prophecies of
Merlin, and the legend of Arthur as they are known today.

✯ EVENTS   Having been repeatedly challenged by rival rulers and
baronial rebellions, and after 18 years of virtually continuous

warfare, Stephen of England is forced to accept Matilda's son, Henry of Anjou, the future Henry II, as his lawful successor.

Establishment of the Plantagenet Dynasty: the name given to the royal dynasty in England from Henry II to Richard II (1154–1399), then continued by two rival houses of younger lines, Lancaster and York, until 1485. The dynasty is so called because, allegedly, Geoffrey of Anjou, father of Henry II, sported a sprig of broom (Old French, *plante genêt*) in his cap.

Nicholas Breakspear becomes the first and only English pope, as Adrian IV.

Thomas à Becket is appointed chancellor to Henry II of England.

1157

✿ BIRTHS   Richard I, 'the Lionheart': King of England, son of Henry II. Of his 10-year reign, he will spend only five months in England, devoting himself to crusading, and defending the Angevin lands in France.

1159

✝ DEATHS   Adrian IV (Nicholas Breakspear): English Pope (1154–9), the only Englishman to hold the office. As Pope, he is said to have granted Ireland to Henry II of England.

1161

✭ EVENTS   Canonization of Edward the Confessor.

1162

✭ EVENTS   Thomas à Becket, chancellor to Henry II of England, is appointed Archbishop of Canterbury.

1163

✭ EVENTS   Edward the Confessor's still undecayed body is moved to a new shrine under the orders of Henry II.

1164

✷ EVENTS   Constitutions of Clarendon: a written declaration of
rights claimed by Henry II of England in ecclesiastical affairs,
with the purpose of restoring royal control over the English
Church. Proclaimed at Clarendon, near Salisbury, the
Constitutions (especially Clause 3, which jeopardizes benefit
of clergy and threatens clerical criminals with secular penalties)
bring Thomas à Becket and Henry II into open conflict:
Becket rejects the Constitutions on the grounds that they
undermine church powers.

Council of Northampton: Becket is found guilty of feudal
disobedience and flees England.

1165

✝ DEATHS   Malcolm IV, the 'maiden': King of Scotland,
grandson of David I.

1167

❀ BIRTHS   John: King of England, son of Henry II. He will be
one of the least popular monarchs in English history.

1169

✷ EVENTS   Strongbow, Earl of Pembroke, invades Ireland and
establishes Anglo-Norman rule.

1170

❀ BIRTHS   Edmund Rich: English prelate and Archbishop of
Canterbury. He will become famous as a preacher.

✝ DEATHS   Thomas à Becket: on his return from exile, he is
murdered in Canterbury Cathedral by four of King
Henry II's knights.

1171

✷ EVENTS   Henry II leads a major expedition to Ireland when
the Earl of Pembroke proclaims himself King of Leinster,
resulting in its annexation.

The cult of Thomas à Becket develops with the recording of 14
miraculous cures at his shrine.

1173

⭐ EVENTS   John and Richard, the sons of Henry II of England, are encouraged by Queen Eleanor to rebel in an alliance with Louis VII of France, William I of Scotland, and Count Philip of Flanders. All parts of the King's dominions are threatened, but his enemies are defeated.

William I of Scotland invades Northumberland during the rebellion against Henry II of England, but is captured at Alnwick.

1174

⭐ EVENTS   Treaty of Falaise: William I of Scotland recognizes Henry II of England as the feudal superior of Scotland.

1176

⭐ EVENTS   Assize of Northampton: judicial reform which divides England into six regions, each with a justice.

1178

⭐ EVENTS   Assize of Arms: reorganizes England's militia.

1185

⭐ EVENTS   Lincoln Cathedral destroyed by an earthquake.

1187

✿ BIRTHS   Prince Arthur: grandson of Henry II.

1189

✝ DEATHS   Henry II (Henry of Anjou): King of England. Dies shortly after facing further disloyalty from his family when his sons, John and Richard I, allied with Philip II of France, who overran Maine and Touraine. Before he dies, Henry agrees a peace which recognizes Richard as his sole heir for the Angevin empire.

⭐ EVENTS   Third Crusade (to 1192): proclaimed by Pope Gregory VIII following the defeat by Saladin of the field army of the Latin Kingdom of Jerusalem at the Battle of Hittin (Jul 1187), and his subsequent capture of the Holy City itself

(Oct 1187). Led by the three great rulers of Western
Christendom, Frederick I, 'Barbarossa', Philip II of France
and Richard I, 'the Lionheart', the Crusade promises much,
but ultimately fails in its objective of regaining Jerusalem.
Richard manages to achieve a compromise settlement whereby
pilgrimage to the Holy Places is safeguarded and the
Crusaders maintain their position in the Levant with the
Muslims (in this case the Ayyubid Dynasty) controlling the
hinterland.

1192

✪ EVENTS   Pope Celestine III declares the Scottish Church free
of all external authority save the Pope's.

On his return from the third crusade, Richard I of England is
captured in Austria and held hostage.

1193

✪ EVENTS   In the absence of Richard I, Hubert Walter, Bishop
of Salisbury and Archbishop of Canterbury becomes justiciar
of England, and is responsible for all the business of
government until his resignation in 1198.

John, son of Henry II, fails in his attempt to seize the crown of
Richard I. He is later forgiven and nominated successor by
Richard, who thus sets aside the rights of Prince Arthur, the
son of John's elder brother, Geoffrey.

1194

✪ EVENTS   Richard I ransomed for 100,000 marks and released.

1198

❁ BIRTHS   Alexander II: King of Scots, son of William I, 'the
Lion'. His reign will represent an important landmark in the
making of the Scottish kingdom.

1199

✝ DEATHS   Richard I, 'the Lionheart': King of England, son of
Henry II. Of his 10-year reign, he spent only five months in
England, devoting himself to crusading, and defending the

Angevin lands in France. He is mortally wounded while
  besieging the castle of Châlus, Aquitaine.

John, youngest son of Henry II, succeeds to the throne of Richard
  I. Hubert Walter becomes chancellor, and is consulted on
  important matters of state. John's oppressive government, and
  failure to recover Normandy, will provoke baronial opposition,
  leading to demands for constitutional reform, and the signing
  of the Magna Carta.

13th Century

The 13th century in Britain witnessed an intellectual development which established Britain's reputation as equal to the continental centres of learning. Central to this was the founding of the two great universities at Cambridge and Oxford. Events such as the Crusades and their ongoing struggle for the Holy Lands put Britain more in harmony with the other Christian powers and harnessed the energy of popular religion. The signing of Magna Carta in 1215 reorganized the handling of power and the position of the monarchy in relation to the constitution.

Art and architecture were very much dominated by the early Gothic style, with the creation of illuminated manuscripts (the most enduring art form of the 1200s) passing from the monasteries to lay artists, allowing, via the universities, a wider appreciation of the works. For the first time, the pointed Gothic arch, flying buttress and ribbed vault came to the fore in architecture. It was in this style that the original Westminster Abbey was constructed from 1245. The latter 1200s saw an inclination away from the Gothic to the Decorated style, which was characterized by the 'ogee' (a double or 'S' curve) and by the use of maximum decoration on all available surfaces.

The music and literature of this century produced less spectacular, but nonetheless enduring creations. In 1225, the first Round (a short melody, normally divided into three for unaccompanied voices with separate points of entry into the song) in English, *Sumer is Icumen In*, was written. The Round was very popular as an informal musical form in which all could participate. A similarly popular form developed in literature, with the Mystery Plays or Miracle Cycles. These were a form of drama, depicting the events of the Bible from the Creation to the Ascension, written in the vernacular and enacted on special occasions. They dealt with serious subjects in a lighthearted manner and were influential in the development of much medieval drama.

1200

✿ BIRTHS   (c.) Matthew Paris: English chronicler and Benedictine monk.

Treaty of Le Goulet: King Philip of France recognizes the French possessions of King John of England in return for John's acceptance of Philip's overlordship in France.

1202

✮ EVENTS   Fourth Crusade (to 1204).

1203

✞ DEATHS   Prince Arthur: grandson of Henry II. On the death of Richard I (1199), Arthur claimed the English Crown. He was supported for a while by the French king, Philip II, but King John eventually has him murdered.

✮ EVENTS   Philip II of France, in support of Arthur, marches against John and seizes most of English-held Aquitaine.

1204

✮ EVENTS   Due to John's murder of Arthur, Philip II of France confiscates Normandy.

1205

✞ DEATHS   Hubert Walter: English churchman, statesman and Bishop of Salisbury.

1206

✮ EVENTS   Pope Innocent III makes Stephen Langton a cardinal.

1207

✿ BIRTHS   Henry III: King of England, son of King John.

✮ EVENTS   John of England refuses to recognize appointment by Pope Innocent III of Stephen Langton as cardinal and Archbishop of Canterbury.

1208

✿ BIRTHS   (c.) Simon de Montfort, Earl of Leicester: English politician and soldier.

✸ EVENTS   John's kingdom is placed under papal interdict.

1209

✸ EVENTS   Innocent III excommunicates King John for attacks on church property and declares him deposed.

1213

✸ EVENTS   King John makes peace with Pope Innocent III, following the threat of a French invasion, making England and Ireland papal fiefs.

1214

❀ BIRTHS   (c.) Roger Bacon: English Franciscan philosopher. Will write on Aristotle's physics and metaphysics, and dedicate himself to experimental science.

✝ DEATHS   William I, 'the Lion', King of Scots, brother and successor of Malcolm IV. Despite his difficulties with England, he made Scotland a much stronger kingdom.

✸ EVENTS   (27 Jul) Battle of Bouvines: English are defeated by the French, and rebellion in England against King John follows.

1215

✸ EVENTS   Magna Carta: the 'Great Charter', imposed by rebellious barons on King John of England. It is designed to prohibit arbitrary royal acts by declaring a body of defined law and custom which the King must respect in dealing with all his free subjects. The principle that kings should rule justly was of long standing, but in Magna Carta the first systematic attempt is made to distinguish between kingship and tyranny. While failing to resolve all the problems raised by the nature of the English crown's relations with the community, it endures as a symbol of the sovereignty of the rule of law, and is of fundamental importance to the constitutional development of England and other countries whose legal and governmental systems are modelled on English conventions.

First of the Barons Wars (to 1217) during the reign of King John: comes about after the sealing of Magna Carta: many barons still defy John, and offer the crown to Prince Louis (later Louis VIII) of France. After John's death, the French and baronial army is routed at Lincoln (May 1217), and the war is effectively ended by the Treaty of Kingston-on-Thames (Sep 1217).

1216

✝ DEATHS   John: King of England, son of Henry II. Dies suddenly of a fever.

1217

✯ EVENTS   Battle of Dover: the French are expelled from England.

1218

✯ EVENTS   Fifth Crusade (to 1221).

1221

✯ EVENTS   First arrival in England of Dominican and Franciscan friars.

1224

✯ EVENTS   Anglo-French war (to 1227).

1227

✯ EVENTS   Edmund Rich is commissioned by Pope Gregory IX to preach the Sixth Crusade throughout England.
Sixth Crusade (to 1229).

1228

✝ DEATHS   Stephen Langton: English prelate and Archbishop of Canterbury.

1234

✯ EVENTS   Edmund Rich appointed Archbishop of Canterbury.

1237

✯ EVENTS   Treaty of York: Alexander II, King of Scots, renounces his hereditary claims to Northumberland,

Cumberland, and Westmorland, and concentrates on the vigorous assertion of royal authority in the north and west.

1239

✿ **BIRTHS**   Edward I, King of England: son of Henry III. Will build a reputation as a crusader, and struggle to quell Scotland and Wales during his reign.

1240

✝ **DEATHS**   Edmund Rich: English prelate and Archbishop of Canterbury.

✭ **EVENTS**   (c.) Great Council adopts the title 'Parliament'.

1241

✿ **BIRTHS**   Alexander III: King of Scotland, son of Alexander II.

1242

✭ **EVENTS**   Henry III unsuccessfully wages war against France in an attempt to regain lost territory.

1245

✭ **EVENTS**   Westminster Abbey: beginning of the replacement of the original building by the present building in early English Gothic style.

1249

✝ **DEATHS**   Alexander II: King of Scots, son of William I, 'the Lion'. His reign was an important landmark in the making of the Scottish kingdom. Dies of a fever on Kerrera, near Oban, while leading an expedition to wrest the Western Isles from Norwegian control.

1250

✿ **BIRTHS**   (c.) John Balliol: King of Scotland. Supported in his claim for the Scottish throne by Edward I of England, against Robert Bruce.

✭ **EVENTS**   Margaret, Scottish queen, wife of Malcolm III, 'Canmore', is canonized.

1254

✴ EVENTS   Henry III is given the Sicilian throne by the pope.

1258

✴ EVENTS   Provisions of Oxford: a baronial programme
imposing constitutional limitations on the English crown.
Henry III of England has to share power with a permanent
council of barons, parliaments meeting three times a year,
and independent executive officers (chancellor, justiciar,
treasurer).

1259

✝ DEATHS   Matthew Paris: English chronicler and Benedictine
monk. Although he concentrated on the history of his own
monastery, St Albans Abbey, he gave in his main work
(*Chronica Majora*) the fullest available account of events in
England between 1236 and 1259, as well as information on
other European countries. He was also noted for his maps
and drawings.

1261

✴ EVENTS   The Pope absolves Henry from his oath to observe
the Provisions of Oxford.

1263

✴ EVENTS   Second Barons War: breaks out after the Provisions
of Oxford fail to achieve a settlement, and some barons led
by Simon de Montfort capture Henry III at Lewes (1264).
Earl Simon is killed at Evesham (1265), and the King is
restored to power by the Dictum of Kenilworth (1266).

1264

✴ EVENTS   (14 May) Battle of Lewes: Henry III defeated by
Simon de Montford.

1265

✝ DEATHS   Simon de Montfort, Earl of Leicester: English
politician and soldier. After defeating Henry III at Lewes
(1264) he became virtual ruler of England, calling a

parliament in 1265. But the barons grew dissatisfied with his rule, and the army of Henry III defeated him at the Battle of Evesham (4 Aug), where he was killed and dismembered.

1266

☆ EVENTS   Dictum of Kenilworth: annuls the Provisions of Oxford.

The Hebrides become part of the Kingdom of Scotland when they are ceded to Alexander III by Magnus of Norway.

1268

☆ EVENTS   The remains of Edward the Confessor are moved yet again.

1272

✟ DEATHS   Henry III: King of England, son of King John.

1274

✿ BIRTHS   Robert Bruce (Robert I): King of Scotland and main figure in Scottish War of Independence.

(c.) William Wallace: Scottish patriot and fighter for Scottish independence.

1275

☆ EVENTS   First of the Statutes of Westminster (also 1285 and 1290): part of a comprehensive programme undertaken by Edward I to reform English law and administration. The first statute is concerned mainly with criminal matters, notably compulsory trial by jury.

1276

☆ EVENTS   First of Edward I's devastating campaigns to annexe Wales (1277).

1277

☆ EVENTS   Henry III's son, Edward I, embarks on conquest of Wales and the Welsh Wars are concluded.

Roger Bacon, English philosopher and scientist, imprisoned for heresy after his writings are condemned by the Franciscans.

1282

❀ BIRTHS Queen Isabella, wife of Edward II of England.

✝ DEATHS Llywelyn ap Gruffudd, Prince of Wales: killed by Edward I.

★ EVENTS Investiture of the title Prince of Wales: in the UK, the title conferred by custom on the sovereign's eldest son. Tradition holds that after the death in battle of Llywelyn ap Gruffudd (the first independent ruler of Wales to be acknowledged by an English king) and the execution of his brother, Edward I presents his own infant son to the Welsh people at Caernarvon Castle as their prince.

1283

❀ BIRTHS Margaret, 'Maid of Norway': infant Queen of Scotland (1286–90). The granddaughter of Alexander III of Scotland, she is the only child of Alexander's daughter, Margaret (who dies in childbirth), and King Erik II of Norway.

Edward Balliol: 'King' of Scotland, son of John Balliol.

1284

❀ BIRTHS Edward II: King of England, son of Edward I.

★ EVENTS Following Edward I's brutal campaign and the defeat and death of Llywelyn in 1282, the English conquest of Wales is complete.

1285

★ EVENTS Second of the Statutes of Westminster (also 1275 and 1290): part of a comprehensive programme undertaken by Edward I to reform English law and administration. The second statute covers many fields of law, and facilitates the creation of entailed estates.

1286

✝ DEATHS Alexander III: King of Scotland, son of Alexander II. Dies after a fall from his horse. Margaret, 'Maid of Norway' (b.1283), the granddaughter of Alexander III, is the only direct survivor of the Scottish royal line.

1289

✴ EVENTS   Margaret, 'Maid of Norway', is betrothed to the
    infant Prince Edward (the future Edward III of England),
    son of Edward I.

1290

✝ DEATHS   Margaret, 'Maid of Norway': infant Queen of
    Scotland (1286–90). Dies at sea on her way from Norway to
    the Orkneys. Her death thwarts the plan to unite the crowns
    of England and Scotland.

✴ EVENTS   Jews expelled from England.

Third of the Statutes of Westminster (also 1275 and 1285): part
    of a comprehensive programme undertaken by Edward I to
    reform English law and administration. The third statute
    protects lords' feudal incidents.

1292

✝ DEATHS   Roger Bacon: English Franciscan philosopher.
    Imprisoned until shortly before his death.

✴ EVENTS   Edward I selects John Balliol from 13 possible
    candidates to succeed to the Scottish throne.

1294

✴ EVENTS   Rebellion breaks out again in Scotland.

1295

✴ EVENTS   A council of 12 of the magnates take control of
    Scottish government out of the hands of the king, John Balliol,
    and conclude an alliance with France, then at war with
    England.

1296

✴ EVENTS   Edward I deposes John Balliol from Scottish throne
    after his renunciation of his homage and moves the Stone of
    Destiny from Scone to Westminster.

(27 Apr) Battle of Dunbar: the battle fought between English
    and Scottish forces after Scottish magnates deprive King John
    (Balliol) of independent authority and negotiate alliances with

France and Norway. Edward I marches north and his victory
results in Balliol's resignation of the throne. He is taken to
England as prisoner. The Scottish War of Independence
ensues, and Scotland remains without a king until Robert
Bruce is crowned in 1306.

1297

★ EVENTS   (11 Sep) Battle of Stirling Bridge: Scots under
   William Wallace defeat the English.

1298

★ EVENTS   (22 Jul) Battle of Falkirk: Edward I's troops defeat
   William Wallace.

14th Century

During the 14th century, Britain struggled against seemingly constant catastrophe and war. The famine of 1315 and plague of 1348 were made worse by civil disturbance during the Anglo-Scots wars and the intermittent bouts of the Hundred Years War (between England and France). The mortality rate following the Black Death caused massive social restructuring, making the peasant workers more valuable and toppling the feudal system.

This social upheaval is very much reflected in the literature of the time. Poets such as Geoffrey Chaucer and John Gower wrote extensively on a wide range of subjects relevant to all levels of society, not just the ruling classes. Chaucer wrote on subjects from politics and religion to courtly love and classical legend. He is, however, probably best known for his uninhibited use of the base and often vulgar humour of his time. Another poet, William Langland, wrote *Piers Plowman*, a poem which is accepted as the masterpiece of the Middle English alliterative revival and deals with the dream vision of a common man. Another classic from this period is *Sir Gawain and the Green Knight* — a tale of chivalry and honour in the life of one of the knights of the Round Table.

The visual arts, particularly architecture, developed strongly in accordance with literature. In architecture, the Decorated style predominant in the 13th century grew into the Perpendicular style, which developed in London in the 1330s. The Perpendicular rejected all the fuss and stylization of the Decorated style and stressed straight lines, slender supports and large windows. The sobriety of this style very much reflected the political and social gravity of the era.

1301

☆ EVENTS   Edward I invests his son, Edward, as first Prince of Wales.

1303

★ EVENTS   Scots, fighting for independence under John Comyn, defeat the English at Roslin.

1304

★ EVENTS   Fall of Stirling Castle leads to the capture of William Wallace and the submission of the Scots.

1305

† DEATHS   William Wallace: Scottish patriot and fighter for Scottish independence. Hung, drawn and quartered in London after his arrest in Glasgow. Quarters distributed to Newcastle, Berwick, Stirling and Perth.

1306

★ EVENTS   During a quarrel with his political rival John Comyn, Robert Bruce stabs him to death; then assembles his vassals and is crowned King of Scotland at Scone. This precipitates a renewed revolt against England.

1307

† DEATHS   Edward I, King of England; son of Henry III. Built a reputation as a crusader, and struggled to quell Scotland and Wales during his reign. Dies marching to war against the Scots.

★ EVENTS   (May) Battle of Loudon Hill: Victory for the Scots under Robert Bruce against the English.

After the death of Edward I, and in the wake of recent Scottish victories, the English are forcibly expelled from the country and all the great castles recovered except Berwick and Stirling.

1309

★ EVENTS   Robert Bruce, King of Scotland, convenes his first Scottish parliament at St Andrews.

1311

★ EVENTS   Ordinances in the court of Edward II restrict the royal prerogative in matters such as appointments to the

King's household, and demand the banishment of Edward's
favourite, Piers Gaveston, who is ultimately captured and
executed (1312).

1312

❀ BIRTHS   Edward III, King of England; son of Edward II.

✪ EVENTS   The Scots under Robert Bruce begin cross border
raids, attacking Durham and Hexham.

1314

✪ EVENTS   Revival of the Anglo-Scots war.

(24 Jun) Robert Bruce declares Scotland independent after
defeating the English under Edward II at the Battle of
Bannockburn. The battle makes Bruce a national hero, and
inspires Scottish counter-attacks against northern England.

1315

✝ DEATHS   John Balliol: once King of Scotland. Supported in
his claim for the Scottish throne by Edward I of England,
against Robert Bruce.

✪ EVENTS   The failure of two successive harvests causes
widespread famine throughout Britain and central and
western Europe.

1316

❀ BIRTHS   Robert II: King of Scotland, grandson of Robert
Bruce.

1318

✪ EVENTS   Berwick falls to the Scots, who now threaten all of
northern England.

Treaty of Leake: imposed by the magnates upon the royal
household with the aim of reforming it to their approval.

1319

✪ EVENTS   Anglo-Scots truce.

1320

★ EVENTS (6 Apr) Declaration of Arbroath: a response by
Scottish barons, with the support of the Church, to a demand
from Pope John XXII that the Scots make peace with England.
The Pope does not recognize Robert Bruce as King of
Scotland. Almost certainly written by Bruce's Chancellor,
Bernard de Linton, also Abbot of Arbroath, the declaration
asserts the separate nationhood of Scotland and the integrity
of its 'uninterrupted succession of 113 Kings, all of our own
native and royal stock'. The declaration, a skilful and effective
piece of anti-English propaganda, declares that the signatories
would never 'consent to subject our selves to the dominion of
the English' and urges the Pope to take note of the wrong
and calamities to the Church and state which had been
wrought by the English incursions. Unsurprisingly, it has
since become a key document for supporters of a separate
Scottish nation.

1321

★ EVENTS Threat of civil war in England, as the king's
favourites, the Despensers, rise to his defence against the
magnates.

1322

★ EVENTS Reversal of the Ordinances in the court of Edward II
which restrict the royal prerogative in matters such as
appointments to the King's household. The king openly
favours Hugh le Despenser and his son, Hugh le Despenser,
the younger, both of whom are greatly unpopular amongst the
magnates in Parliament.

1323

★ EVENTS Anglo-Scots 13-year truce is agreed.

1324

❀ BIRTHS David II: King of Scotland, son of Robert Bruce.

1325

❀ BIRTHS   (c.) John Gower: English poet.

1326

✦ EVENTS   Queen Isabella and her lover Roger Mortimer stage a rebellion, executing both the Despensers, then imprisoning Edward II in Kenilworth Castle.

1327

✝ DEATHS   Edward II: renounces the throne in favour of his eldest son, Edward III, and shortly afterwards is murdered in Berkeley Castle, near Gloucester.

✦ EVENTS   Treaty of Corbeil: Franco-Scots alliance re-established.

1328

✦ EVENTS   Treaty of Northampton: Edward III of England recognizes the independence of Scotland and Robert Bruce's right to the throne.

1329

✝ DEATHS   Robert Bruce (Robert I): King of Scotland, main figure in Scottish War of Independence. Dies of leprosy. Succeeeded by his son, David Bruce (David II).

1330

❀ BIRTHS   Edward the Black Prince: son of Edward III. Earns his name from his black armour.

(c.) John Wycliffe: English religious reformer.

✝ DEATHS   Roger Mortimer: lover of Isabella of France. Having helped Isabella to overthrow and murder her husband, Edward II, he is executed by her son, Edward III. Isabella is imprisoned for life.

1331

✦ EVENTS   David Bruce (David II) crowned King of Scotland, aged only seven.

1332

✿ BIRTHS   (c.) William Langland: English poet, author of *Piers Plowman*.

✭ EVENTS   Edward Balliol invades Scotland and has himself crowned King at Scone.

Edward Balliol flees following an attack by supporters of his rival, David Bruce.

1333

✭ EVENTS   Edward III of England invades Scotland.

(19 Jul) Battle of Halidon Hill: a battle between England and Scotland during the Scottish Wars of Independence. Edward III of England turns from besieging Berwick-upon-Tweed, inflicts a massive defeat on the Scottish relief army and restores to Edward Balliol the title King of Scots.

1334

✭ EVENTS   David Bruce (David II) flees to exile in France.

1336

✭ EVENTS   Renewed English invasion of Scotland.

1337

✭ EVENTS   Beginning of Hundred Years War between France and England (to 1435).

A series of wars between England and France forming part of a longer contest which begins when England is linked with Normandy (1066), then with Anjou and Aquitaine (1154). In the 13th century, the French Capetian kings redouble their efforts to rule all France, but when Edward III claims the French throne, from 1340 styling himself 'King of England and France', traditional rivalries explode into a dynastic struggle. Under Henry V (1415/22) the English turn from raiding to territorial conquest, a task ultimately beyond their resources. Eviction from Guyenne (1453) reduces England's French territories to Calais (lost in 1558) and the Channel Islands, but the title of King of France is abandoned only in 1801.

Institution of the Duchy of Cornwall, the oldest of the English Duchies, by Edward III, to provide support for his eldest son, Edward the Black Prince.

1340

❀ BIRTHS   John of Gaunt: Duke of Lancaster, son of Edward III. Influential as a peacemaker during the reign of Richard II.

(c.) Robert III, King of Scotland, son of Robert II.

✴ EVENTS   (24 Jun) Battle of Sluys: English naval victory under Edward III against superior French fleet.

1341

✴ EVENTS   David II of Scotland returns from exile.

1342

❀ BIRTHS   (c.) Julian of Norwich: English mystic, author of *Revelations of Divine Love*, an influential work stressing the power of the love of God.

1344

✴ EVENTS   (c.) Establishment of the Most Noble Order of the Garter: the oldest and highest order of chivalry in Europe, founded by Edward III of England. Its emblem is a blue garter, edged in gold and inscribed with *Honi soit qui mal y pense* (French: 'Shame on him who thinks evil of it'), traditionally the words spoken by Edward after he picks up the Countess of Salisbury's dropped garter.

1345

❀ BIRTHS   (c.) Geoffrey Chaucer: English poet, author of *The Canterbury Tales*.

1346

✴ EVENTS   (26 Aug) Battle of Crécy: a battle between France and England in the Hundred Years War. Using tactics perfected against the Scots, Edward III routs a larger French army, mainly cavalry, near Abbeville (Somme). It is a classic demonstration of the superiority over mounted knights of a co-ordinated force of dismounted men-at-arms, and archers providing offensive fire-power.

(4 Sep) Battle of Neville's Cross: the Scots are beaten back at Durham, and the English take David II hostage (to 1357).

1348

★ EVENTS   Black Death reaches England (to 1349): virulent bubonic and pneumonic plague that sweeps through west and central Europe from Asia (1347–51). It is later estimated that the population of England in 1400 was approximately half that of a century earlier, and that about 1,000 villages were destroyed or depopulated. With the reduction of labour available to cultivate the land, land-owners are forced to offer wages in place of the old feudal traditions to keep their tenants and this, coupled with generally higher rates charged by the remaining craftsmen and traders, brings the possibility of social change to a hitherto strictly stratified society.

1350

❀ BIRTHS   (c.) Owen Glendower: Welsh rebel.

★ EVENTS   Black Death reaches Scotland.

1351

★ EVENTS   Labourers' Statute: a law passed in an endeavour to stabilize the English economy in the wake of the Black Death. It represents the first ever attempt to control wages and prices by freezing wages and the prices of manufactured articles, and by restricting the movement of labour. Like most subsequent attempts, it fails abysmally to achieve its aims and is a significant factor in the 1381 Peasants' Revolt.

1356

★ EVENTS   (19 Sep) Battle of Poitiers: a battle between England and France during the Hundred Years War. The English forces, under Edward the Black Prince (son of Edward III), are victorious and King John II of France is captured. The battle has important consequences, with the French king agreeing to return all possessions in France which were held by Henry II of England. When the French nobility resist these

terms, Edward III invades France and lays siege to Paris.
Edward Balliol resigns his claim to the Scottish throne.

1357

✯ EVENTS   David II of Scotland released from English captivity.

1358

✝ DEATHS   Queen Isabella, wife of Edward II of England.

1360

✯ EVENTS   The Treaty of Bretigny (1360), which cedes much
territory in France to Edward III together with a large ransom
for King John II of France. It represents one of the high points
of English success during the Hundred Years War.

1361

✯ EVENTS   Second outbreak of plague in England.

1363

✯ EVENTS   Merchant Staplers: a group of 26 English merchants
who are granted exclusive royal authority to export wool to
the continent via the staple port of Calais (where the wool
market is concentrated), in return for which they lend money
to English monarchs. The value of the monopoly declines
with the rise of cloth exports, and the rising cost of maintaining
the Calais garrison.

1364

✝ DEATHS   Edward Balliol: 'King' of Scotland, son of John
Balliol.

1366

❀ BIRTHS   Henry IV (Henry Bolingbroke): first English king
from the House of Lancaster, son of John of Gaunt.

1367

❀ BIRTHS   Richard II: King of England, son of Edward the Black
Prince.

1369

✯ EVENTS   Third outbreak of plague in England.

1371

♱ DEATHS   David II: King of Scotland, son of Robert Bruce.

✯ EVENTS   Robert II of Scotland becomes first Stuart monarch
(to 1390).

1375

✯ EVENTS   Treaty of Bruges: agreement of one year Anglo-
French truce.

1376

♱ DEATHS   Edward the Black Prince: son of Edward III. Earned
his name from his black armour.

✯ EVENTS   Renewal of the Treaty of Bruges for a second year.

1377

✿ BIRTHS   Henry Beaufort: English cardinal and political figure.

♱ DEATHS   Edward III: King of England, son of Edward II.

✯ EVENTS   Imposition of the Poll Tax for the first time (a fixed
tax levied on each member of the population).

1378

✿ BIRTHS   (c.) Sir John Oldcastle: English knight and Lollard
leader. After being convicted for heresy, he will escape and
stage an abortive uprising against Henry V.

1379

✯ EVENTS   Imposition of a second Poll Tax.

1380

✯ EVENTS   Third Poll Tax levied at three times the rate of the
1377 tax.

1381

✮ EVENTS   Peasants' Revolt in England: an English popular
rising, among townsmen as well as peasants, based in Essex,
Kent, and London, with associated insurrections elsewhere.
It is precipitated by the three oppressive poll taxes of 1377–
81, the underlying causes being misgovernment, the desire for
personal freedom, and an assortment of local grievances. It
is dealt with by Richard II who personally confronts the masses
to hear their part, and quickly suppresses the revolt.

1382

✮ EVENTS   Statute de Heretico Comburendo: in an attempt to
crush heresy, the statute forbids unlicensed preaching and
allows for the burning of unyielding heretics.

Founding of Winchester College, Hampshire.

1384

✝ DEATHS   (c.) John Wycliffe: English religious reformer. He was
sent to Bruges to treat with ambassadors from the Pope about
ecclesiastical abuses, but his views were found unacceptable,
and he was prosecuted. He then attacked the Church
hierarchy and the doctrine of transubstantiation, wrote many
popular tracts in English (as opposed to Latin), and issued
the first English translation of the Bible. His opinions were
condemned, and he was forced to retire to Lutterworth,
where he wrote prolifically until his death. The characteristic
of his teaching was its insistence on inward religion in
opposition to the formalism of the time. His followers were
known as 'Lollards', and the influence of his teaching was
widespread in England, in many respects anticipating the
Reformation. Dies after having a stroke in mass.

✮ EVENTS   Expulsion of the Lollards from Oxford following
Wycliffe's death.

1386

✮ EVENTS   Appointment of the Council of 11, to whom the king
is compelled to entrust the government of England.

1387

❀ BIRTHS   Henry V: King of England, son of Henry IV. His reign
         will focus upon the quelling of the Welsh rebels and his claim
         to the French crown.

1389

❀ BIRTHS   John of Lancaster, Duke of Bedford: English general
         and statesman, son of Henry IV.

✯ EVENTS   Three year Anglo-French truce.

1390

❀ BIRTHS   John Dunstable: English composer and early
         exponent of counterpoint.

✞ DEATHS   Robert II: King of Scotland, grandson of Robert
         Bruce.

✯ EVENTS   Fourth outbreak of plague in England.

1391

❀ BIRTHS   Humphrey, Duke of Gloucester, son of Henry IV, and
         protector during the minority of Henry VI.

1394

❀ BIRTHS   James I: King of Scotland, son of Robert III.

1397

✯ EVENTS   Richard II proclaims himself absolute monarch.

1398

✯ EVENTS   Henry Bolingbroke is banished by Richard II, first
         for ten years, subsequently for life.

1399

✞ DEATHS   John of Gaunt, Duke of Lancaster, son of Edward
         III. Was influential as a peacemaker during the reign of
         Richard II.

✯ EVENTS   After John of Gaunt's death, his estates are declared forfeit to Richard II. John's son, Henry Bolingbroke, returns despite his banishment to claim his inheritance and subsequently induces Richard to concede the crown. Henry is then instated as Henry IV.

15th Century

During the 15th century, culture in Britain and, indeed, across the whole of Europe was dominated by the onset of the early Renaissance period in Italy. British painters, sculptors and architects were inspired by the superior work of their Italian counterparts, such as Donatello, Brunelleschi, Michelangelo and Botticelli.

Music in Britain in the 1400s was more influential than influenced. The English composer John Dunstable is credited with having a major impact on the development of the continental (especially French and Italian) composers who succeeded him. He wrote principally church and mass music, and refined the system of counterpoint (the combining of two or more melodies into one). At about the same time, the English musician Henry Abyndon was the first to take a degree in music, from Cambridge in 1464.

For the world of literature and writing, the 15th century was a crucial turning point. By 1430, modern English had developed out of Middle English and was gradually adopted as the standard for writers. The development of printing in Britain opened new doors for literature and learning. The first book printed in England was produced in 1474 by William Caxton and Chaucer's *Canterbury Tales* were in print three years later. Writers of prominence in the 1500s, such as Robert Henryson, William Dunbar, John Skelton and Thomas Malory, could look forward to the revolution brought by the printing press.

1400

✝ DEATHS Richard II, King of England: after having been deposed by Parliament, apparently murdered at Pontefract Castle.

Geoffrey Chaucer: English poet, author of *The Canterbury Tales*.

William Langland: English poet, author of *Piers Plowman*.

✯ EVENTS   Owen Glendower of Wales rebels against English.

Henry IV defeated after attacking Scotland. Henry Percy
(Hotspur) and his house then join with the Scots and the
Welsh against him.

1401

✯ EVENTS   Persecution of the Lollards: John Wycliffe's religious
sect is accused of heresy.

1403

✯ EVENTS   Henry Percy (Hotspur) defeated (along with Owen
Glendower) and killed at Battle of Shrewsbury (21 Jul) by
Henry IV.

1405

✯ EVENTS   Welsh rebellion against Henry IV.

1406

♰ DEATHS   Robert III, King of Scotland, son of Robert II.

✯ EVENTS   James (later James I of Scotland), son of Robert III,
is captured by the English and held prisoner for 18 years
before being released and beginning his reign.

1407

✯ EVENTS   Formation of the Merchant Adventurers: a small
company of local guilds that export woollen cloth from
London, first to the Netherlands and later to Germany. They
increasingly dominate trade, have headquarters in Antwerp
from 1496 and, as woollen cloth is England's leading export,
are important in economy and finance until the mid-17th
century.

Fifth outbreak of the plague in England.

1408

♰ DEATHS   John Gower: English poet.

✯ EVENTS   (Feb) Battle of Branham Moor: the Earl of
Northumberland is defeated and executed after successive
rebellions against Henry IV.

1410

✷ EVENTS   Conclusion of Owen Glendower's ultimately
unsuccessful 10 year revolt against the English crown.

1413

✝ DEATHS   Henry IV (Henry Bolingbroke): King of England,
first of the House of Lancaster, son of John of Gaunt. Dies
of a stroke while in prayer.

Julian of Norwich: English mystic, author of *Revelations of Divine
Love*, an influential work stressing the power of the love of
God.

✷ EVENTS   Sir John Oldcastle is convicted of heresy due to his
Lollard involvement, but escapes from the Tower.

1414

✷ EVENTS   Sir John Oldcastle conspires with other Lollards to
capture Henry V at Eltham Palace, Kent, and take control of
London. The rising is abortive, and Oldcastle flees.

1415

✷ EVENTS   (25 Oct) Battle of Agincourt: the first battle of the
second stage of the Hundred Years War, between France and
England. Henry V of England is forced to fight near Hesdin
(Pas-de-Calais) by the French who, ignoring the lessons of
the Battles of Crécy and Poitiers (1356), pitch cavalry against
dismounted men-at-arms and archers. Though heavily
outnumbered, the English win an overwhelming victory, and
return in 1417 to begin the systematic conquest of Normandy.

1416

✝ DEATHS   (c.) Owen Glendower: Welsh chief. Rebelled against
Henry IV in 1400, fighting for Welsh independence.

1417

✝ DEATHS   Sir John Oldcastle: English knight and Lollard leader.
After being convicted for heresy, he escaped and staged an
abortive uprising against Henry V in 1413. Although he fled
at the time, he was eventually caught, hanged and burnt.

★ EVENTS (4 Sep) Battle of Caen: Henry V of England claims victory over the French.

1419

★ EVENTS English under Henry V take control of Normandy.

1420

★ EVENTS Treaty of Troyes: completes English conquest of Normandy. Henry V is recognized as heir to the French throne and Regent of France and marries Catherine of Valois, daughter of Charles VI.

1421

❀ BIRTHS Henry VI: King of England, son of Henry V.

1422

❀ BIRTHS (c.) William Caxton: the first English printer.

✝ DEATHS Henry V: King of England, son of Henry IV. Dies of dysentery.

★ EVENTS John of Lancaster succeeds his brother, Henry V, as Guardian of England and Regent of France.

Third stage of the Hundred Years War commences.

1423

★ EVENTS (23 Aug) Battle of Verneuil: Anglo-Burgundian force defeats Franco-Scottish.

1424

★ EVENTS After 18 years captivity in England, James I returns to Scotland.

1425

❀ BIRTHS (c.) Robert Henryson: Scottish poet.

1427

★ EVENTS Henry Beaufort is sent as papal legate to Germany

to organise a crusade against the heretical Hussites, but fails
and falls from papal favour.

1428

❀ BIRTHS   Richard Neville, Earl of Warwick, ('the Kingmaker'):
   English soldier and politician.

✦ EVENTS   Siege of Orléans (to 1429): the English blockade of
   the main stronghold still loyal to Charles VII of France,
   during the Hundred Years War.

1429

❀ BIRTHS   Margaret of Anjou: Queen Consort of Henry VI of
   England, daughter of René of Anjou.

✦ EVENTS   (28 Apr) The English are defeated at Orléans by a
   French force under Joan of Arc.

1430

❀ BIRTHS   James II: King of Scotland, son of James I.

1431

✦ EVENTS   Hundred Years War: Henry VI of England crowned
   King of France.

The English burn Joan of Arc as a witch at Rouen.

1435

✟ DEATHS   John of Lancaster, Duke of Bedford: English general
   and statesman, son of Henry IV. During the campaigns of his
   brother, Henry V, against France he was appointed Lieutenant
   of the Kingdom. After Henry's death (1422), he became
   Guardian of England and Regent of France.

✦ EVENTS   Congress of Arras: Anglo-French conference to
   discuss settlement of the Hundred Years War. English refuse
   the French's offer to cede Normandy and Guienne if the
   English claim to the French throne is renounced.

1437

✟ DEATHS   James I: King of Scotland, son of Robert III. He is
   murdered at Perth by a group of noble supporters of the

House of Stuart, against whom James is ruthless. This is the first assassination of a Scottish king for 400 years.

1440

✦ EVENTS   Founding of Eton College, Berkshire.

1442

✿ BIRTHS   Edward IV, King of England, son of Richard, Duke of York.

1447

✝ DEATHS   Henry Beaufort: English cardinal and political figure.

Humphrey, Duke of Gloucester, son of Henry IV, and protector during the minority of Henry VI. He greatly increased the difficulties of his brother, Bedford, by his greed, irresponsibility, and factious quarrels with their uncle, Cardinal Henry Beaufort. He was arrested for high treason at Bury St Edmunds and five days later was found dead in bed. It is unclear if the circumstances were natural or suspicious.

1450

✝ DEATHS   Jack Cade (birth date unknown): Irish leader of the rebellion against Henry VI (see below).

✦ EVENTS   Rebellion against Henry VI: assuming the name of Mortimer and the title of Captain of Kent, Jack Cade marches on London with c.40,000 followers, demanding government reform and the return of the Duke of York to power. A promise of pardon results in discord among the insurgents, and they disperse. A price is put on Cade's head, and he is killed in Sussex while trying to reach the coast.

(15 Apr) Battle of Formigny: the decisive defeat near Bayeux (Calvados) during the Hundred Years War of an army sent by the English government, then bankrupt and bereft of allies, to stem French advances in Normandy. Having lost their previous tactical superiority, the English are bombarded out of their positions by artillery, and routed by infantry. The French reconquest of Normandy is swiftly completed.

1452

✿ BIRTHS   Richard III, King of England; son of Richard, Duke
   of York.

James III: King of Scots, son of James II of Scotland.

1453

✝ DEATHS   John Dunstable: English composer and early
   exponent of counterpoint.

✭ EVENTS   (17 Jul) Battle of Chatillon: English cease attempts
   to conquer France after the loss of their final French territory,
   Guyenne (Guienne) to the French. Marks the end of Hundred
   Years War.

1454

✭ EVENTS   Richard, Duke of York, seizes power as Lord
   Protector from the mentally ill Henry I.

1455

✭ EVENTS   (22 May) Richard, Duke of York, defeats the king's
   army at St Albans, the first battle of the Wars of the Roses.

Wars of the Roses (to 1485): a series of civil wars in England,
   which start during the weak monarchy of King Henry VI;
   named from the emblems of the two rival branches of the
   House of Plantagenet, York (white rose) and Lancaster (red
   rose); a symbolism propagated by the Tudor Dynasty (1485–
   1603), which unites the two roses. The wars begin when
   Richard, Duke of York, claims the protectorship of the crown
   after the King's mental breakdown (1454), and effectively
   end with Henry Tudor's defeat of Richard III at Bosworth
   Field (1485) and his marriage to Elizabeth of York (1486).
   The armies are small and the warfare intermittent, although
   marked by brutal executions. The wars are not purely dynastic
   in origin, and are exacerbated by the gentry and by aristocratic
   feuds, notably between the Neville and the Percy Family, and
   by the unstable 'bastard feudal' system, in which relations
   among landed élites are increasingly based upon self-
   interest — a system that the Tudors seek to control.

1457

✿ BIRTHS   Henry VII (Henry Tudor): first Tudor King of
England.

1459

✭ EVENTS   Fighting resumes in the Wars of the Roses.

1460

✿ BIRTHS   (c.) William Dunbar: Scottish poet.

(c.) John Skelton: English satirical poet and court poet to
Henry VII.

✝ DEATHS   James II, King of Scotland: killed by cannon
explosion during siege of Roxburgh Castle.

Henry, Duke of York, is killed at Battle of Wakefield.

✭ EVENTS   (10 Jul) Battle of Northampton: Henry VI is taken
hostage by the victorious Yorkists under the Earl of Warwick.

1461

✭ EVENTS   (17 Feb) Second Battle of St Albans: Queen Margaret
defeats the Yorkists and releases her husband, Henry VI.

Henry VI is deposed by Edward, Duke of York, who succeeds
him as Edward IV.

1464

✭ EVENTS   Henry VI returns from exile in Scotland to lead the
Lancastrian cause, but is captured and imprisoned (1465–
70).

Plague epidemic again strikes Britain.

1470

✿ BIRTHS   Edward V, King of England, son of Edward IV.

✭ EVENTS   Earl of Warwick defeats Edward IV, forcing him into
exile in Holland, and restores Henry VI to the English throne.
His nominal rule ends when Edward IV returns to London
(Apr 1471).

1471

☦ DEATHS   Richard Neville, Earl of Warwick, ('the Kingmaker'):
English soldier and politician. He exercised great power
during the first phase of the Wars of the Roses, championing
the Yorkist cause. In 1460 he defeated and captured Henry
VI at Northampton, had his cousin, Edward, Duke of York,
proclaimed King as Edward IV, and then destroyed the
Lancastrian army at Towton. When Edward tried to assert his
independence, Warwick joined the Lancastrians, forcing the
King to flee to Holland, and restoring Henry VI to the throne.
He is defeated and killed by Edward IV at the Battle of Barnet
(14 Apr).

Henry VI, King of England, son of Henry V. Murdered in the
Tower of London during course of Wars of the Roses. He
had suffered from periodic bouts of madness from 1453, and
during his reign the French conquests of Henry V had been
progressively eroded.

Sir Thomas Malory (birth date unknown): English writer,
author of *Le Morte D'Arthur.*

★ EVENTS   (4 May) Battle of Tewkesbury: a decisive battle in the
Wars of the Roses at which Edward IV defeats Lancastrian
forces hastily assembled by Queen Margaret, wife of Henry
VI. Their son, Prince Edward, is killed as are many other
leading Lancastrian supporters. Soon afterwards, Edward IV
is able to re-enter London, order the death of Henry VI in
the Tower of London and resume his reign, which is not
thereafter seriously challenged. Margaret is imprisoned in the
Tower for four years until ransomed by Louis XI of France.

Incorporation of Orkney and Shetland, the Vikings' longest held
overseas settlement, within the Scottish realm due to the
marriage (in 1469) of James III of Scotland to Margaret of
Denmark.

1473

❀ BIRTHS   James IV: King of Scotland, son of James III.

1474

✿ **BIRTHS**   (c.) Sebastian Cabot: explorer and navigator, son of John Cabot.

1475

✿ **BIRTHS**   (c.) Thomas Wolsey: English cardinal and statesman.

✯ **EVENTS**   William Caxton prints the first book in English, the *Recuyell of the Historyes of Troye*, which he translates himself.

1478

✿ **BIRTHS**   Sir Thomas More: statesman, scholar and English Lord Chancellor.

1482

✝ **DEATHS**   Margaret of Anjou: Queen Consort of Henry VI of England, daughter of René of Anjou. Because of Henry's madness, she became deeply involved in political life, and during the Wars of the Roses was a leading Lancastrian.

✯ **EVENTS**   Recapture of Berwick-upon-Tweed from the Scots by Richard III of England.

1483

✝ **DEATHS**   Edward IV, King of England.

Edward V and Richard, Duke of York, sons of Edward IV: known as the 'Princes in the Tower' after their uncle, Richard, Duke of Gloucester interred them in the Tower of London and they were never seen again; probably murdered on Richard's orders.

✯ **EVENTS**   When Edward IV dies and is succeeded by his under-age son, Edward V, Richard, Duke of Gloucester, acts first as protector; within three months he has himself proclaimed and crowned as the rightful King.

1485

✝ **DEATHS**   Richard III, King of England: defeated and killed at Battle of Bosworth Field by Henry Tudor.

☆ EVENTS   (22 Aug) Battle of Bosworth Field: the battle which puts Henry Tudor on the English throne (as Henry VII) after victory over Richard III.

Establishment of the Tudor dynasty: the name of the ruling house of England from Henry VII's overthrow of Richard III to the death of Elizabeth I in 1603. The Tudors were originally a North Wales gentry family, one of whose descendants married a Plantagenet in the early 15th century, elevating the family to the peerage.

1486

☆ EVENTS   Henry VII marries Elizabeth of York, thus uniting the Houses of York and Lancaster; end of Wars of the Roses.

1487

☆ EVENTS   Henry VII founds what is subsequently known as the Court of the Star Chamber as a supplement to regular courts of law.

1488

❀ BIRTHS   Miles Coverdale: English Protestant reformer and biblical scholar.

♱ DEATHS   James III: King of Scots, son of James II of Scotland. Defeated and killed by rebel nobles at the Battle of Sauchieburn, near Stirling (11 Jun).

1490

☆ EVENTS   Renewal of the Franco-Scots alliance, binding Scotland to attack England if she is at war with France.

1491

❀ BIRTHS   Henry VIII: King of England, son of Henry VII.

♱ DEATHS   (c.) William Caxton: the first English printer. He learned the art of printing, probably in Cologne (1471–2), and printed the first book in English, the *Recuyell of the Historyes of Troye* (1475). He then set up his wooden press in Westminster (c.1476), and produced the *Dictes* or *Sayengis of the Philosophres* (1477), the first book printed in England. Of about 100 books printed by him, including the *Canterbury Tales*, over a third survive only in unique copies or fragments.

1492

✭ EVENTS   Henry VII, first Tudor King of England, concludes peace with France.

1494

✭ EVENTS   Poynings' Law: statutes enacted by the Irish parliament at the direction of English Lord Deputy Sir Edward Poynings, removing its right to meet or pass laws without the agreement of the English government. The immediate aim is to suppress Yorkist support, but it ultimately helps English claims to sovereignty.

1497

✭ EVENTS   Exploring under the patronage of Henry VII of England, the Venetian navigator, John Cabot, sights land (probably Cape Breton Island, Nova Scotia) and claims North America for England.

1499

✭ EVENTS   Outbreak of plague in Scotland.
Renewal of the Anglo-Scots truce.

16th Century

The 16th century saw the development of the struggle between Catholicism and Protestantism, Reformation and Counter-Reformation. Central to this struggle was the relationship between Henry VIII and the Catholic Church in Rome. In 1521, Henry was created Defender of the Faith by Pope Leo X for his defence of the Catholic Church against Lutheranism, but by 1538, following his unpopular marriage to Anne Boleyn, his proclamation of himself as supreme head of the church in England and the dissolution of the monasteries, he was excommunicated.

British art was influenced by these religious developments and also by the Netherlandish and German schools represented by artists such as Bosch, Dürer and Holbein (later court artist for Henry VIII) which flourished alongside the artistic developments of the Italian Renaissance. In architecture there was, around the middle of the century, a movement towards the Elizabethan style. This was characterized by symmetrical façades, Netherlandish decoration, over-sized windows and E- or H-shaped floor plans.

Music in the 1500s was dominated by two very influential musicians and composers: William Byrd and Thomas Tallis. Byrd — considered the greatest of the Tudor composers — was a devout Catholic, but at this time he wrote for both Catholic and Anglican services, as well as composing madrigals and music for strings. Much of his life was spent in partnership with Tallis, 'the father of cathedral music', with whom, in the early 17th century, he was granted a monopoly on printing music.

Britain's strong literary tradition continued with the work of writers who are, to this day, recognized as masters of their craft. The most obvious and dominant of these is William Shakespeare, who wrote the majority of his works between 1580 and 1600. Writing comedy, tragedy and history, he drew his inspiration from a vast array of sources, making all of his tales seemingly timeless and very much his own. Shakespeare, along with his contemporary Marlowe, brought the language of his drama and poetry into everyday vocabulary in Britain, influencing not only future generations of writers but also the character of the English language.

1501

✭ EVENTS   Arthur, the eldest son of Henry VII, marries Catherine of Aragon but dies the following year.

1503

❀ BIRTHS   Sir Thomas Wyatt: English courtier and poet.

✭ EVENTS   Marriage of James IV of Scotland to Margaret Tudor, the eldest daughter of Henry VII: an alliance which leads ultimately to the union of the crowns.

1505

❀ BIRTHS   Thomas Tallis: English musician, known as 'the father of cathedral music'.

1508

✝ DEATHS   (c.) Robert Henryson: Scottish poet.

1509

✝ DEATHS   Henry VII (Henry Tudor): First Tudor King of England. As King, he restored peace and prosperity to the country, which was helped by his marriage of reconciliation with Elizabeth of York. He was also noted for the efficiency of his financial and administrative policies.

✭ EVENTS   Henry VIII marries Catherine of Aragon, the widow of his brother Arthur, and cements an alliance with Spain.

1511

✭ EVENTS   The warship, *Mary Rose*, is built for Henry VIII.

1512

❀ BIRTHS   James V, King of Scotland, son of James IV.

1513

❀ BIRTHS   (c.) John Knox: Protestant reformer.

✝ DEATHS   James IV, King of Scotland, is killed by the English at the Battle of Flodden.

✴ EVENTS   (9 Sep) Battle of Flodden: a victory of the English over the Scots, fought in Northumberland. James IV of Scotland, allied with France, invades England, a signatory of the Holy League against France, but is defeated by English forces under Thomas Howard, Earl of Surrey. The Scottish dead include James, 13 earls, and three bishops; the battle ends the Scottish threat for a generation.

(16 Aug) Battle of the Spurs, won by Henry VIII on his invasion of France.

1516

❀ BIRTHS   Mary I (Mary Tudor), Queen of England, daughter of Henry VIII and Catherine of Aragon.

1518

✴ EVENTS   Foundation of the Royal College of Physicians by Thomas Linacre, physician to Henry VII and Henry VIII.

1520

✝ DEATHS   (c.) William Dunbar: Scottish poet.

1521

✴ EVENTS   Henry VIII of England made 'Defender of the Faith' by Pope Leo X for his opposition to Luther and defence of Catholic sacraments.

1526

✴ EVENTS   Sebastian Cabot explores the coast of South America for Charles V, but fails to colonize the area, and is imprisoned then banished to Africa. He later returns to England where he is made inspector of the navy by Edward VI.

1529

✝ DEATHS   John Skelton: English satirical poet, court poet to Henry VII.

★ EVENTS   Henry VIII begins process of divorcing Catherine of Aragon and starts cutting ties with Church of Rome. This leads directly to the Reformation in England, the process by which the English Church rejects the authority of the Roman Catholic Church and establishes its own doctrine and liturgy with an emphasis on the sovereignty of God and the translation of God's word into the vernacular.

Hampton Court, the royal residence situated by the River Thames near London, becomes the residence of British monarchs for over two centuries.

1530

✝ DEATHS   Thomas Wolsey: English cardinal and statesman. As Lord Chancellor for Henry VIII he was the king's leading adviser and was in charge of day-to-day running of government. Following his evasive behaviour over Henry's divorce from Catherine of Aragon, he lost the king's favour and was impeached and arrested for high treason. He dies en route to London following his arrest.

1532

★ EVENTS   Sir Thomas More, English Lord Chancellor, resigns over the issue of Henry VIII's divorce.

1533

❀ BIRTHS   Elizabeth I, Queen of England and Ireland, daughter of Henry VIII and Anne Boleyn.

(c.) David Rizzio: Italian courtier and musician in service of Mary, Queen of Scots.

★ EVENTS   Henry VIII marries Anne Boleyn, a marriage Pope Clement VII refuses to recognize.

1534

★ EVENTS   Act of Supremacy: put into effect by Thomas

Cromwell, Earl of Essex, it makes Henry VIII supreme head
of the church in England.

1535

✟ DEATHS   Sir Thomas More, statesman, scholar and English
Lord Chancellor: beheaded by Henry VIII for refusing to
take Oath of Supremacy and accept Henry as the head of the
English Church.

(c.) Wynkyn de Worde (birth date unknown): London printer,
pupil of William Caxton; he succeeded to Caxton's business
in 1491. He made great improvements in printing and
typecutting, and was the first in England to use italic type.

1536

✟ DEATHS   Anne Boleyn, Henry VIII's second wife, is beheaded
for adultery. Henry marries Jane Seymour shortly afterwards.

✷ EVENTS   Act of Union joins England and Wales.

Dissolution of the Monasteries begins in England (to 1540),
effected by Thomas Cromwell following Henry VIII's
assertion of himself as head of church.

Pilgrimage of Grace (to 1537): a major Tudor rebellion in
England directed against the religious and secular policies of
Henry VIII, especially the Dissolution of the Monasteries.

Henry VIII appoints Hans Holbein, 'the Younger', as court
painter.

1537

❀ BIRTHS   Edward VI, King of England and Ireland, son of
Henry VIII and Jane Seymour.

Lady Jane Grey, Queen of England for nine days.

(c.) 4th Earl of Bothwell (James Hepburn): Scots nobleman and
third husband of Mary, Queen of Scots.

✟ DEATHS   Jane Seymour, Henry VIII's third wife, dies, leaving
behind an infant son.

1538

✴ EVENTS   Pope Paul III issues Bull of excommunication and deposition against Henry VIII.

1539

✴ EVENTS   First court house is erected at the Old Bailey.

1540

❀ BIRTHS   (c.) Hugh O'Neill (2nd Earl of Tyrone): Irish rebel who will fight for an independent Ireland.

(c.) Sir Francis Drake: English navigator.

William Gilbert: English physician, who discovered the natural magnetism of the earth and was the first to use the term 'electricity'.

✴ EVENTS   Henry VIII marries Anne of Cleves. Six months later the marriage is annulled and Henry marries Catherine Howard.

1541

✴ EVENTS   In response to the Protestant reformation, the Catholic church begins new reform and missionary activity known as the 'Counter-Reformation'.

1542

❀ BIRTHS   Mary, Queen of Scots, daughter of James V.

✝ DEATHS   James V, King of Scotland.

Sir Thomas Wyatt: English courtier and poet, whose poems helped to introduce the Italian sonnet and other forms into English literature.

Henry VIII's fifth wife, Catherine Howard, is beheaded for sexual indiscretions.

✴ EVENTS   (24 Nov) Battle of Solway Moss: a victory for the English over the Scots.

Following the death of James V, his week-old daughter, Mary, becomes Queen of Scots (to 1567).

1543

❀ BIRTHS   William Byrd: Tudor composer.

✷ EVENTS   Henry VIII marries Catherine Parr, his sixth, and
    final, wife.

1544

✷ EVENTS   Henry VIII and Charles V of Spain invade France.

1545

✷ EVENTS   Henry VIII's warship, *Mary Rose*, sinks in action off
    Portsmouth.

1547

✝ DEATHS   Henry VIII: King of England.

✷ EVENTS   (10 Sep) Battle of Pinkie: a victory for the English
    over the Scots.

   Henry VIII gives the Bethlehem Royal Hospital (Bedlam) to the
   City of London as a lunatic asylum. It is notorious for
   centuries for the cruelty inflicted upon its inmates.

1549

✷ EVENTS   Acts of Uniformity: first of a series of acts (to 1662)
    passed by English parliaments which sought to impose
    religious uniformity by requiring the use of the Church of
    England liturgy as contained in the Book of Common Prayer.

1550

❀ BIRTHS   John Napier: Scottish mathematician.

   (c.) Henry Hudson: English navigator.

✷ EVENTS   Founding of Sherborne School, Dorset.

1552

❀ BIRTHS   (c.) Edmund Spenser: English poet.

   Richard Hakluyt: English geographer.

   Sir Walter Raleigh: English courtier, navigator and author.

✱ EVENTS   Second Act of Uniformity: as with the original act,
aims to impose religious uniformity via the use of Church of
England liturgy as contained in the Book of Common Prayer.

1553

✝ DEATHS   Edward VI, King of England and Ireland: dies of
tuberculosis, aged only 16.

✱ EVENTS   On death of Edward VI, Lady Jane Grey rules as
Queen of England for nine days before being deposed and
beheaded by Edward's Catholic sister Mary Tudor. Mary
becomes Queen Mary I of England.

1554

❀ BIRTHS   Sir Philip Sydney: English poet.

✱ EVENTS   Mary I of England marries Philip II, heir to the
Spanish throne.

Foundation of the Muscovy Company (to 1649): an English
trading company. It is granted a charter allowing it to
monopolize trade between England and Russia.

Second Act of Repeal: removes all anti-papal measures instituted
since 1529.

1555

✱ EVENTS   England returns to Roman Catholicism, with Mary
I repealing anti-Catholic legislation and reviving Catholic
practices with the aim of restoring papal supremacy. Results
in approximately 300 Protestants being burned at the stake.

1556

✱ EVENTS   Plantation of Ireland: the colonization and conquest
of Ireland (to 1660) by English and Scottish settlers. The
policy leads to rebellions by the native Irish and Anglo-Irish
aristocracy and the eventual conquest of Ireland under
Cromwell. Results in the deaths of approximately two-thirds
of the Irish population.

1557

✿ BIRTHS   (c.) Thomas Morley: English composer.

✝ DEATHS   Sebastian Cabot: explorer and navigator, son of John Cabot.

1558

✿ BIRTHS   Thomas Kyd: English dramatist.

✝ DEATHS   Mary I (Mary Tudor), Queen of England.

✵ EVENTS   England loses Calais, last English possession in France.

With ascent of Elizabeth I to the English throne, Catholic legislation is repealed in England.

Reformation in Scotland: process by which papal authority is repudiated and Protestant forms of worship and doctrine are established. Influential are Elizabeth I of England and John Knox who reject Catholicism in favour of Protestantism despite the opposition of Mary, Queen of Scots.

1559

✵ EVENTS   Act of Supremacy, by which Elizabeth I becomes supreme governor of the English church.

1560

✵ EVENTS   Puritanism: beginning of the movement calling for further reformation of the Church of England arising out of dissatisfaction with supposedly 'popish elements', such as surplices, which had been retained in the church by the Elizabethan settlement. Lacking in coherence, it is more a collection of opinions and personalities than an organized movement.

Reformation in Scotland: John Knox introduces the Presbyterian Church of Scotland.

1561

✿ BIRTHS   Francis Bacon: English philosopher and statesman.

✵ EVENTS   John Knox's 'Book of Discipline' lays down new Scottish church constitution.

1562

★ EVENTS   Hugh O'Neill leads unsuccessful Irish rebellion
against the English. John Hawkins becomes the first
Englishman to traffic slaves between West Africa and the West
Indies.

1563

❀ BIRTHS   John Bull: English organist and composer, credited
with composing *God Save the King*, one of the founders of
contrapuntal keyboard music.

1564

❀ BIRTHS   William Shakespeare: English dramatist and poet.
Christopher Marlowe: English dramatist.

1565

★ EVENTS   Introduction of tobacco to Britain by Walter Raleigh.

1566

❀ BIRTHS   James VI of Scotland (from 1567) and I of England
(from 1603, following the Union of the Crowns), son of
Mary, Queen of Scots.

✟ DEATHS   David Rizzio: Italian courtier and musician in the
service of Mary, Queen of Scots. Murdered by a group of
nobles led by Darnley, Mary's husband, who is jealous of his
position with the queen and his growing political power.

1567

✟ DEATHS   Lord Darnley, husband of Mary, Queen of Scots. His
house is blown up while he is bedridden with smallpox, and
he seems to have been strangled while trying to escape. The
Earl of Bothwell, a recent favourite of the Queen's, is the
most probable suspect.

★ EVENTS   Following Darnley's murder, Mary marries Bothwell,
is forced to abdicate and is imprisoned by her nobility. After
escaping and raising an army, she is again defeated and takes

refuge in England (1568) where she is imprisoned by
Elizabeth I. Her infant son is declared King James VI of
Scotland.

Foundation of Rugby School, England, a public school for boys;
traditionally, the game of rugby football is said to have
originated here.

1568

✝ DEATHS   Miles Coverdale: English Protestant reformer and
biblical scholar. His own translation of the Bible (the first
complete one in English) appeared in 1535.

1569

★ EVENTS   Rebellion of the Northern Earls: led by the Catholic
earls of Westmoreland and Northumberland in support of
Catholicism and the release of Mary, Queen of Scots.

1570

❀ BIRTHS   Guy Fawkes: English conspirator and main player in
the Gunpowder Plot to blow up James I and his ministers in
the Houses of Parliament.

1571

★ EVENTS   Founding of Harrow School, Middlesex.

1572

❀ BIRTHS   Ben Jonson: English dramatist.

(c.) John Donne: English poet and Dean of St Paul's.

✝ DEATHS   John Knox: Protestant Reformer.

★ EVENTS   Francis Drake becomes the first Englishman to see
the Pacific ocean.

1573

❀ BIRTHS   William Laud: English prelate and Archbishop of
Canterbury.

Inigo Jones: English architect, founder of classical English
architecture and introducer of the Palladian style to England
from Venice.

1577

✯ EVENTS   Sir Francis Drake sets off around the world in the *Golden Hind*.

1578

❀ BIRTHS   William Harvey: English physician.

✝ DEATHS   4th Earl of Bothwell (James Hepburn): Scots nobleman and third husband of Mary, Queen of Scots. Having fled to Scandinavia after Mary's overthrow, he is imprisoned and dies, insane, in Denmark.

1580

❀ BIRTHS   (c.) John Webster: English dramatist.

✯ EVENTS   Sir Francis Drake returns to England having successfully circumnavigated the globe.

1583

❀ BIRTHS   Orlando Gibbons: English composer.

1584

❀ BIRTHS   (c.) William Baffin: English navigator.

✯ EVENTS   Walter Raleigh sends an expedition to America to claim lands for Elizabeth I (to 1549).

1585

✝ DEATHS   Thomas Tallis: English musician, known as 'the father of cathedral music'.

1586

✝ DEATHS   Sir Philip Sydney: English poet.

✯ EVENTS   Introduction of the potato to Britain by Walter Raleigh.

1587

✝ DEATHS   Mary, Queen of Scots: executed for treason by Elizabeth I of England.

✯ EVENTS   England at war with Spain; Drake destroys Spanish fleet at Cadiz.

1588
❀ BIRTHS   Thomas Hobbes: English political philosopher.
✯ EVENTS   Spanish Armada is defeated off Portsmouth. This gives Britain new opportunity for world trade and colonization.

1591
❀ BIRTHS   Robert Herrick: English poet.

1593
✝ DEATHS   Christopher Marlowe: English dramatist. Dies after being fatally stabbed in a tavern brawl.

1594
✝ DEATHS   Thomas Kyd: English dramatist.

1595
✯ EVENTS   Foundation of the Bodleian Library and national depository at Oxford, by Sir Thomas Bodley.

1596
✝ DEATHS   Sir Francis Drake: English navigator. Dies of dysentery on expedition to the West Indies.

1597
✯ EVENTS   Second Spanish Armada leaves for England but is scattered by storms.

Second Irish rebellion under Hugh O'Neill.

Transportation: introduction of sentence of banishment from England to America, and later Australia, for those convicted of certain offences. Most of the convicts are young, poorly-educated urban-dwellers convicted of some form of theft. In the early years of settlement, convict labour is used on public works; subsequently, the typical fate of most convicts is assignment to private service. Practice continues into 1860s.

1598

✮ **EVENTS**   Poor Laws: legislation whereby relief of poverty becomes the responsibility of individual parishes under the supervision of Justices of the Peace and the administration of Overseers. Funds are provided by local property rates. The initial laws lay down the basis for foundation of Workhouses and punishment of beggars.

Beginning of construction of the Globe Theatre on Bankside in London, with Shakespeare as a shareholder.

1599

✾ **BIRTHS**   Oliver Cromwell: English soldier and Lord protector of England.

✝ **DEATHS**   Edmund Spenser: English poet.

✮ **EVENTS**   Irish rebels defeat English army led by the Earl of Essex.

17th Century

The 17th century was a period of constant change in British history. The political crises of the civil wars, the shock of a king's execution, Restoration and Glorious Revolution touched the lives of everyone and as a result were reflected in all aspects of the creative arts.

In architecture, the prevailing influence running through the century came from the Flemish schools. The Jacobean period was not radically distinct from the preceding Elizabethan; its architecture was characterized by late Gothic influence with classical details. Designer Inigo Jones was the first to introduce to Britain the Renaissance classical architectural style and to establish Palladian ideas.

Furniture design moved from a predominance of heavy oak, Jacobean pieces to the Dutch-influenced William and Mary style which was more intimate, with more elegant designs featuring delicate ornamentation.

Painting and sculpture were, if anything, rather overshadowed by the achievements of the other fields. There were no truly outstanding artists, and those who did shine were predominantly foreign-born or strongly influenced by foreign schools. During this period, the Dutch were unsurpassed.

The turbulent political scene had a strong influence on literature, which was often dark and preoccupied with evil, the comic represented by satire. The Cavalier poets, for example, Robert Herrick, were a group of gentlemen poets loyal to King Charles I who adhered to semi-chivalric ideals centring around love and war. After the civil wars, the Restoration period spawned English literature's classical Augustan age, with the exploration of new forms familiar in modern writing, such as the novel, biography and travel writing. Satirical poetry — a key element in any period of political flux — developed from Dryden through Swift to Pope. In addition, there was a considerable vogue for heroic plays and comedies of manners.

1600

✿ BIRTHS   Charles I: King of England, Scotland and Ireland, son of James VI (of Scotland) and I (of England).

★ EVENTS   East India Company establishes a trading monopoly in India with trading stations at Surat, Madras, Bombay and Calcutta.

As part of his anti-Puritan policy, James VI establishes bishops in Scotland.

1601

★ EVENTS   Second Irish rebellion quelled.

Poor Law Act formalizes all earlier Poor Law legislation.

1602

♱ DEATHS   Thomas Morley: English composer.

★ EVENTS   Expulsion of the Jesuits from England.

1603

♱ DEATHS   Elizabeth I: Queen of England and Ireland, daughter of Henry VIII.

William Gilbert: English physician, who discovered the natural magnetism of the earth and was the first to use the term 'electricity'.

★ EVENTS   Union of the Crowns: James VI of Scotland becomes James I of England; first Stuart king of England.

1604

★ EVENTS   Treaty of London: brings peace between England and Spain after the defeat of the Spanish Armada.

1605

★ EVENTS   Gunpowder Plot to blow up British Parliament discovered. The scheme reflects Catholic despondency after the failure of previous plots to remove James I in 1603. Peace

with Spain in 1604 ended the prospect of foreign support,
and new anti-Catholic sanctions led to desperate measures
being taken by the Catholic community.

Britain's first railway is constructed in Nottinghamshire.

1606

❀ BIRTHS   William Davenant: English poet and playwright.

✝ DEATHS   Guy Fawkes: English conspirator and key player in
the Gunpowder Plot to blow up James I and his ministers in
the Houses of Parliament. He is hanged after being caught
red-handed.

★ EVENTS   Establishment of the Virginia Company, a joint stock
company to promote English settlement in North America.

1608

❀ BIRTHS   John Milton, English poet.

1609

★ EVENTS   Henry Hudson, English navigator, discovers the
Hudson River while in search of a passage across the North
Pole.

1610

★ EVENTS   Bodleian Library, Oxford, henceforth receives a free
copy of every book published in England.

1611

✝ DEATHS   Henry Hudson: English navigator, who discovered
the Hudson River while in search of the North Pole. Dies
travelling through the bay and straits which now bear his name
after his crew mutiny and cast him adrift.

★ EVENTS   Plantation of Ulster: English and Scottish Protestant
colonists settle in Northern Ireland.

Parliament dissolved for the first time by James I.

1613

★ EVENTS   Globe Theatre is destroyed by fire and rebuilt.

1614

✿ BIRTHS   Henry More: English philosopher and poet.

✪ EVENTS   The Addled Parliament is dissolved by James I, who calls no subsequent Parliament for seven years.

1616

✿ BIRTHS   Nicholas Culpeper: British physician and astrologer.

✝ DEATHS   Hugh O'Neill (2nd Earl of Tyrone): Irish rebel who fought for an independent Ireland. Dies suddenly while planning attack on Cromwellian army.

William Shakespeare: English dramatist and poet.

Richard Hakluyt: English geographer, who wrote on navigation and introduced the use of globes to schools.

✪ EVENTS   William Baffin discovers Baffin Bay.

1617

✝ DEATHS   John Napier: Scottish mathematician, inventor of logarithms to simplify computation.

1618

✪ EVENTS   Book of Sports: a statement issued by James I specifying which sports may be played on Sundays.

✝ DEATHS   Sir Walter Raleigh: English courtier, navigator and author, and a favourite of Elizabeth I. He introduced tobacco and the potato to Britain and was twice imprisoned in the Tower of London (1592 by Elizabeth; 1603–16 by James I, who eventually had him executed).

1620

✪ EVENTS   A group of English religious dissenters cross the Atlantic in the *Mayflower* to establish the Plymouth colony.

1621

✿ BIRTHS   Andrew Marvell: English metaphysical poet.

Thomas Willis: English physician and founding member of the Royal Society.

★ EVENTS   William Alexander, 1st Earl of Stirling, is granted
    Nova Scotia, the three Atlantic provinces and the Gaspe
    Peninsula as a colony for Scotland. However, the scheme
    meets with a counter-claim for some of the territory by France
    and with few willing settlers the colony ultimately lapses to
    the French.

1622

❀ BIRTHS   Henry Vaughan: Welsh religious poet.

✝ DEATHS   William Baffin: English navigator, who discovered
    Baffin Island while in search of the Northwest Passage. Dies
    during the siege of Ormuz.

1623

✝ DEATHS   William Byrd: Tudor composer.

1625

✝ DEATHS   James VI and I: King of Scotland (from 1567) and
    England (from 1603, with the Union of the Crowns); son of
    Mary, Queen of Scots.

    (c.) John Webster: English dramatist.

    Orlando Gibbons: English composer.

1626

✝ DEATHS   Francis Bacon: English philosopher and statesman.
    Dies after catching cold while conducting an experiment on
    the effect of cold on preservation of flesh.

1627

❀ BIRTHS   Robert Boyle: Anglo-Irish physician.

1628

✝ DEATHS   John Bull: English organist, composer and founding
    member of the Royal Society. Credited with composing *God
    Save the King*.

1629

★ EVENTS   Charles I rules Britain without calling Parliament (to 1640), following the summoning and dissolution of four Parliaments between 1625–9. Period is known as the 'Personal Rule'.

Massachusetts Bay Company: a joint stock company is established by royal charter to promote trade and colonization along the Merrimack and Charles rivers in New England. Its Puritan stockholders settle in Salem and Boston, making the company synonymous with the Massachusetts Bay Colony.

1630

✾ BIRTHS   Charles II: King of England and Scotland, son of Charles I.

1631

✾ BIRTHS   John Dryden: English poet.

John Lower: English physician and physiologist.

✝ DEATHS   John Donne: English poet and Dean of St Paul's.

1632

✾ BIRTHS   Christopher Wren: English architect.

John Locke: English empiricist philosopher.

★ EVENTS   Charles I appoints the Flemish painter Anthony Van Dyck court artist.

1633

✾ BIRTHS   James VII and II: King of Scotland and England.

Samuel Pepys: English naval administrator and diarist.

1634

★ EVENTS   Without Parliament, Charles I introduces Ship Money, a tax on maritime counties and seaports apparently to be used to raise a fleet.

1635

✯ EVENTS   Charles I begins to levy Ship Money from inland
    towns also.

1637

✟ DEATHS   Ben Jonson: English dramatist.

1638

✯ EVENTS   Signing of the National Covenant in Greyfriars
    Churchyard, Edinburgh. Signatories oppose attempts to
    impose English liturgical practice on the Scots church, and
    pledge full support to the Reformed religion and
    Presbyterianism.

1639

✯ EVENTS   The Bishops Wars (to 1640): between Charles I of
    England and the Scottish Covenanters, a group formed by
    the signatories of the National Covenant. The Covenanters
    resist the idea of the Divine Right of Kings and object to the
    attempted imposition of Episcopalianism upon the
    Presbyterian Church of Scotland. Charles I is defeated in the
    wars, and as a result is made bankrupt, forced to call the Short
    and the Long Parliaments and to end the period of his
    'Personal Rule'.

1640

✯ EVENTS   Charles I calls the Short Parliament in an attempt to
    get it to vote for supplies for his Scottish campaign. It refuses
    to do so and is dissolved, creating a basis for the grievances
    felt by the Long Parliament.

Long Parliament is called by Charles I after his defeat in the
    Bishops Wars. It is officially active until 1660 but does not
    meet continually. It is a fairly radical body which attacks
    abuses by the king and his ministers and ultimately abolishes
    the monarchy and the House of Lords.

1641

✯ EVENTS   Catholic revolt in Ireland; massacre of Protestants in
    Ulster.

Beginning of the English Civil War: Parliament abolishes many royal prerogatives and executes Charles I's chief adviser, Lord Strafford. The 'Grand Remonstrance', a statement of the abuses of Charles I and the reforms of the Long Parliament, are published as an appeal for support against the king by a Parliament already split into Royalist and Parliamentary factions.

The Triennial Act requires Parliament to meet at least once every three years as a reaction to Charles I's 'Personal Rule'.

1642

✿ BIRTHS   Sir Isaac Newton: English scientist and mathematician.

✪ EVENTS   War begins when Charles I raises the royal standard at Nottingham. Supporters of Charles I are labelled 'Cavaliers' to describe swaggering courtiers with long hair and swords, while the Parliamentarians are called 'Roundheads' in recollection of the short-haired apprentices who mobbed Charles I at Strafford's trial.

(23 Oct): Battle of Edgehill is the first major engagement of the war and ends inconclusively, although it does allow the Royalists to threaten London, the Parliamentarians' key stronghold.

Introduction of Income and Property tax.

All theatres are closed until 1660.

1643

✪ EVENTS   The Solemn League and Covenant unites the Parliamentarians with the Scots, making Parliament into a formidable military force.

(20 Sep): First Battle of Newbury. Parliamentarians inflict crushing defeat upon the Royalists.

Westminster Assembly: a body of clerics and laymen convened by the Long Parliament to arrange a religious settlement which will replace the Church of England.

1644

✪ EVENTS (2 Jul): Battle of Marston Moor. Parliamentary forces
led by Oliver Cromwell and Prince Rupert and aided by the
Scots are victorious over the Royalists. This leads to the
collapse of the Royalist stronghold of York.

(27 Oct) Second Battle of Newbury. Royalist victory allows the
rescue of Donnington Castle.

Globe Theatre is demolished by the Puritans.

1645

☦ DEATHS William Laud: English prelate and Archbishop of
Canterbury. Beheaded for treason after his policies in
Scotland led to the Bishops Wars.

✪ EVENTS New Model Army created to boost parliament's
cause.

(2 Feb): Battle of Inverlochy sees the defeat of Covenanters by
Royalist Highlanders.

(14 Jun): Parliamentary victory at Battle of Naseby brings
Cromwell and his 'Ironsides' (his cavalry) to the fore as the
main Royalist army is destroyed.

(13 Sep): Battle of Philiphaugh results in the defeat and
destruction of the Scots Royalist forces.

Foundation of the Royal Society of London for the Promotion
of Natural Knowledge (chartered 1660). It is now the UK's
oldest and most prestigious scientific institution.

1646

❀ BIRTHS John Flamsteed: English astronomer and first
Astronomer Royal.

✪ EVENTS (1 May): First Civil War comes to an end after
Charles surrenders to the Scots at Battle of Newark. Attempts
at negotiation between the two sides continually falter over
the issue of religion.

1647

✪ EVENTS Charles is taken into Parliamentary custody, then
seized by the army, who present him with the 'Heads of

Proposals' demanding religious toleration and parliamentary control of the armed forces.

The Levellers, a radical political movement, develop. They call for the extension of manhood franchise to all but the poorest; religious toleration; and the abolition of the monarchy and the House of Lords. They are supported mainly by 'agitators' in the parliamentary army.

1648

✮ EVENTS   Due to a secret alliance with Charles I in which he promises Presbyterianism in England, the Scots invade England, precipitating the Second Civil War.

(17–20 Aug): Battle of Preston brings final victory to Parliament and collapse of Charles's second war after the Scots are repulsed. In total, the two wars cost the lives of one in 10 adult males.

Oliver Cromwell suppresses Catholic rebellion in Ireland.

'Pryde's Purge' of conservative and moderate 'Presbyterian' elements of the Long Parliament considerably reduces its numbers, transforming it into the Rump Parliament.

1649

❀ BIRTHS   James, Duke of Monmouth, English claimant to the throne, born in Amsterdam: the illegitimate son of Charles II.

✝ DEATHS   Charles I, King of England, Scotland and Ireland: executed at Whitehall by Parliamentarians.

✮ EVENTS   Following the King's execution, the monarchy and House of Lords are abolished. Oliver Cromwell establishes the Republican Commonwealth. Although the Commonwealth fails to implement peace in England, Cromwell's armies manage to quell Scotland and Ireland.

Establishment of the Diggers, a radical group preaching agrarian communism on common and waste land. Their initial community at St George's Hill in Surrey spawns other communities in nine counties but the movement is eventually suppressed and crushed by local landowners.

1649–60

☆ EVENTS   Interregnum: period without monarchic rule.

1650

❀ BIRTHS   William of Orange (William III): King of England,
Scotland and Ireland with Mary II.

(c.) Thomas Savery: English engineer, builder of the first
practical steam engine.

☆ EVENTS   (3 Sep): Battle of Dunbar. Cromwell's army defeats
a Scots force supporting Charles II.

Navigation Acts (to 1696): British legislation which aims to
increase England's share of overseas carrying trade by stating
that all imports to England must come in English ships or in
those of the country of origin.

1651

☆ EVENTS   Following the execution of Charles I, his son is
crowned Charles II at Scone.

(3 Sep): Battle of Worcester. Charles's invasion of England is
defeated and leads to his nine year exile in France.

1652

✝ DEATHS   Inigo Jones: English architect, founder of classical
English architecture and introducer of the Palladian style to
England from Venice.

☆ EVENTS   First of three Dutch wars (to 1654) between England
and the Dutch Republic over the issues of trade and the
colonies.

1653

☆ EVENTS   Oliver Cromwell becomes Lord Protector of England
(to 1659) due to the Instrument of Government, England's
only written constitution. This allows Cromwell, as Lord
Protector, to issue ordinances and control the armed forces,
subject to the advice of a Council of State and with parliament
as legislative partner. It fails to maintain support, and its
collapse leads to the Restoration.

Barebones Parliament: institutes civil marriage and seeks legal reforms, but collapses after only six months due to disagreements over abolition of tithes and lay patronage in church.

1654

✝ DEATHS   Nicholas Culpeper: British physician and astrologer, who created the basis for practise of herbalism.

1656

❀ BIRTHS   Edmond Halley: English astronomer and mathematician.

1657

✝ DEATHS   William Harvey: English physician, discoverer of the facts about the circulation of the blood.

1658

❀ BIRTHS   William Paterson: Scottish financier and founder of the Bank of England.

✝ DEATHS   Oliver Cromwell: English soldier and Lord Protector of England.

1659

❀ BIRTHS   Henry Purcell: English composer.

1660

❀ BIRTHS   Daniel Defoe: English writer.

George I: King of Great Britain and Ireland, great-grandson of James I, first of the Hanoverian line.

★ EVENTS   Monarchy is restored under Charles II at the request of the Convention Parliament, following the collapse of the Protectorate regime. Many royal prerogative powers and institutions are not restored.

1661

★ EVENTS   Clarendon Code (to 1665): A series of acts passed by the Cavalier Parliament which reassert the supremacy of the Church of England over Protestant nonconformity after the collapse of the 'Puritan Revolution' in 1660. The most important are the Corporation Act (1661) and the Act of Uniformity (1662). Nonconformity is recognized as lawful, but severe restrictions are placed on the activities of Nonconformists.

First raising of the Horse Guards, an élite regiment of the British army.

1662

✿ BIRTHS   Mary II: Queen of England, Scotland and Ireland with William III, daughter of James VII (of Scotland) and II (of England).

★ EVENTS   Act of Uniformity: part of a series of acts seeking to impose religious uniformity by requiring the use of Church of England liturgy as contained in the Book of Common Prayer. This particular act excludes dissenting Protestant clergy.

1664

✿ BIRTHS   Sir John Vanbrugh: English playwright and Baroque architect. Designer of Castle Howard and Blenheim Palace.

★ EVENTS   Second of three Dutch wars (to 1667) between England and the Dutch Republic over the issues of trade and the colonies.

Beginning of the Great Plague of London (to 1666). Approximately 75,000 people die in London and the disease then spreads widely across England. This is, however, England's last epidemic of plague; after 1667 it spontaneously disappears.

Conventicle Act: prevents groups of more than five worshipping together unless they are Anglicans.

1665

✿ BIRTHS   Anne, Queen of Great Britain and Ireland, daughter of James VII (of Scotland) and II (of England).

1666

★ EVENTS   Great Fire of London. A fire starts in the house of the King's baker in Pudding Lane and spreads rapidly, engulfing 80 per cent of the city. Approximately 13,000 houses, most of the civic buildings and Old St Paul's Cathedral are destroyed, although there are no more than 20 casualties.

(28 Nov): Battle of Pentland Hills: uprising by the Covenanters is brutally crushed.

1667

⚜ BIRTHS Jonathan Swift: Anglo-Irish Clergyman and satirist.

★ EVENTS   Peace of Breda ends war between England, France and the Netherlands.

The Society of Friends, a Christian sect, is formally organized. Sect members are known as 'Quakers' and persecution leads one of their members, William Penn, to establish a Quaker colony in North America, known as Pennsylvania (1681).

1668

✝ DEATHS   William Davenant: English poet and playwright who was responsible for the revival of drama after it was banned by Oliver Cromwell, and for bringing Britain's first public opera to the stage.

★ EVENTS   Triple alliance of England, Sweden and the Netherlands against France.

1670

★ EVENTS   Treaty of Dover: covert treaty between Charles II of Britain and Louis XIV of France, by which it is agreed that Charles will receive French subsidies in return for British amity with the French and later, will declare himself a convert to Roman Catholicism.

Establishment of the Hudson's Bay Company: a London-based corporation which is granted a Royal Charter to trade (principally in furs) in most of north and west Canada.

1671

⚜ BIRTHS   Rob Roy MacGregor: Scottish outlaw.

1672

❀ **BIRTHS**   Joseph Addison: English poet and essayist.

★ **EVENTS**   Third of three Dutch wars (to 1674) between England and the Dutch Republic over the issues of trade and the colonies.

1673

✝ **DEATHS**   Thomas Willis: English physician. Pioneer of study of the anatomy of the brain, cerebral circulation and diseases of the central nervous system.

★ **EVENTS**   Test Act prevents Roman Catholics and Nonconformists from filling public offices in England.

1674

❀ **BIRTHS**   Jethro Tull: English agriculturist, inventor of the seed drill which plants seeds in a row.

✝ **DEATHS**   Robert Herrick: English poet.
John Milton: English poet.

1675

★ **EVENTS**   Building of St Paul's Cathedral (to c.1710): a baroque cathedral on Ludgate Hill in London built by Christopher Wren to replace the medieval cathedral destroyed in the Great Fire of London.

1676

❀ **BIRTHS**   Sir Robert Walpole: English statesman.

1677

★ **EVENTS**   William of Orange, *stadholder* of the Netherlands, marries Mary, heir to the English throne.

1678

✝ **DEATHS**   Andrew Marvell: English metaphysical poet. His death is rumoured to be the result of poisoning after he wrote anti-monarchist tracts, but is actually due to the ignorance of his physician.

✯ EVENTS   Popish Plot in England: Titus Oates and Israel Tonge
           falsely allege existence of a Catholic plot to assassinate Charles
           II of England, burn London, slaughter Protestants, and place
           James, Duke of York (later James VII of Scotland and II of
           England), on the throne. It results in 35 executions, bills in
           three parliaments for the exclusion of James from the
           succession, and the fall of the Danby government.

1679

✝ DEATHS   Thomas Hobbes: English political philosopher.

✯ EVENTS   Act of Habeas Corpus in England forbids
           imprisonment without trial.

Emergence of the Tory party in support of the succession to the
throne of James, Duke of York. The party develops after the
Glorious Revolution (1688) as the champions of the divine
right of monarchy, and has particular support from the country
squirearchy and most sections of the Anglican Church. It
disagrees with religious toleration for Catholics and
Dissenters. At the same time, the opposing Whig party arises.
They uphold the exclusion of James, Duke of York, on the
grounds of his Catholicism and defend the principles of
limited monarchy and the importance of parliament. Whig
support comes mainly from moneyed landowners and from
Nonconformists seeking religious toleration.

(1 Jun): Battle of Bothwell Bridge: Monmouth suppresses the
Covenanters.

1683

❀ BIRTHS   George II: King of Great Britain and Ireland, son of
           George I.

✯ EVENTS   Rye House Plot: an alleged plot by Whigs to murder
           Charles II of England and James, Duke of York, at Rye House
           near Hoddesdon, Hertfordshire. A counterpart to the alleged
           Popish Plot of 1678, it is foiled by the early departure of the
           royal pair from Newmarket. The conspirators are betrayed
           and captured; two of them, Algernon Sidney and William,
           Lord Russell, are executed.

1685

❀ BIRTHS   (c.) Allan Ramsay: Scottish poet.

✟ DEATHS   Charles II: King of England and Scotland. Succeeded
   by his brother, James, Duke of York (James VII of Scotland
   and II of England).

   James, Duke of Monmouth, the illegitimate son of Charles II, is
   beheaded on Tower Hill, after his rebellion against James II
   is brought to an end at the Battle of Sedgemoor (5 Jul).

★ EVENTS   Bloody Assizes: the name given to the western circuit
   assizes in England in the summer of 1685, presided over by
   Lord Chief Justice George Jeffreys after the defeat of the Duke
   of Monmouth at the Battle of Sedgemoor. About 150 of
   Monmouth's followers, mostly farmers and cloth workers, are
   executed, and 800 transported to the West Indies.

1687

✟ DEATHS   Henry More: English philosopher and poet.

★ EVENTS   James VII (of Scotland) and II (of England) issues
   Declaration of Liberty of Conscience; extends toleration to
   all religions.

1688

❀ BIRTHS   Alexander Pope: English satirical poet.

   James Francis Edward Stuart, the 'Old Pretender', son of James
   VII and II. Claimant to the British throne.

★ EVENTS   England's 'Glorious Revolution': William of Orange
   invited by influential Protestants to save England from
   Roman Catholicism; James VII (of Scotland) and II (of
   England) flees to France. Bill of Rights establishes
   constitutional monarchy in England; William III (of Orange)
   and Mary II establish joint monarchy over England and
   Scotland.

   Declaration of Rights: effectively ensures that monarchs must
   operate with the consent of parliament, and must not suspend
   or dispense with laws passed by that body.

   Origination of Lloyd's, an international association of insurance underwriters, in Edward Lloyd's coffee house in the City of London.

1689

✿ BIRTHS   Samuel Richardson: English novelist.

✵ EVENTS   (17 Jul) Battle of Killiecrankie: William III (of Orange) defeated by supporters of James VII (of Scotland) and II (of England).

King William's War (to 1695): the first of the Anglo-French wars over the control of North America. Alternatively known as the War of the League of Augsburg.

1690

✵ EVENTS   (1 Jul) Battle of the Boyne: William III (of Orange) defeats exiled James VII (of Scotland) and II (of England) in Ireland. The battle is celebrated in Northern Ireland as a victory for Protestantism.

1691

✟ DEATHS   Robert Boyle: Anglo-Irish physician and founding member of the Royal Society, who discovered 'Boyle's Law' which states that the pressure and volume of a gas are inversely proportionate.

John Lower: English physician and physiologist. He pioneered blood transfusion and, following William Harvey, recognized the heart as a muscular pump.

1692

✵ EVENTS   (19–20 May) Battle of La Hogue: Anglo-Dutch fleet defeats French fleet, ending French chances of invading Britain.

Massacre of 37 members of the Clan MacDonald by Clan Campbell in Glencoe, Scotland. Alexander MacDonald of Glencoe delayed his submission to an oath of allegiance until 31 Dec 1691, the day before the deadline imposed by the government, and is thus unable to swear until 6 Jan, when a magistrate visits Fort William to receive his oath. The order for punishment is issued, however, and troops lodging with the MacDonalds suddenly fall upon their hosts. Many escape, but the chief is slain along with several men, women and children. A long-standing enemy of the MacDonalds, John Campbell, Earl of Breadalbane, is suspected of planning the attack.

1694

✝ DEATHS   Mary II: Queen of England, Scotland and Ireland with William III. Dies of smallpox.

★ EVENTS   Foundation of the Bank of England, the official government bank in Britain, by William Paterson. It controls the supply of money; prints notes and mints coins; acts as banker to the government and other banks; and manages the gold and currency reserves.

Triennial Act limits the duration of any parliament to three years maximum.

1695

✝ DEATHS   Henry Vaughan: Welsh religious poet.

Henry Purcell: English composer.

★ EVENTS   Foundation of the Bank of Scotland.

1697

★ EVENTS   Newly built St Paul's Cathedral is consecrated and reopened.

1699

★ EVENTS   Disbanding Act: standing army is reduced to 7,000 men.

18th Century

The 18th century was a period of transition which saw the transfer
of political power in Britain from the monarchy to parliament. It
was a century characterized by the conflict of old powers with new,
illustrated by the Jacobite rebellions and the revolt of the 13
American colonies which gave them their independence from
Britain.

In art, portrait painting as practised by Allan Ramsay and Henry
Raeburn was very popular, and impressive landscape works were
produced by Joshua Reynolds and Thomas Gainsborough. The
Royal Academy was founded in 1768, providing a focus for the arts
in Britain. As science progressed, art began looking closely at nature,
influencing the works of Romantic artists such as Turner and
Constable who were to figure strongly into the next century.

Architecture exerted a new influence on interior design in this period,
with inspiration coming from many styles (eg Baroque, Palladian,
Rococo, Chinese, Gothic). Eventually Robert Adam's neoclassicism
(a style characterized by pure geometric form and restrained
decoration) emerged as dominant. By the end of the 18th century,
neoclassicism was at its most refined, reflected in the work of
furniture designer Thomas Chippendale and potter Josiah
Wedgwood.

The novel developed in this century, with authors such as Daniel
Defoe, Samuel Richardson, James Hogg and Henry Fielding
exploring new social topics and investigating the psychological
complexities of human nature and beliefs. Innovations in narrative
technique (as in the work of Laurence Sterne) meant the novel very
much overshadowed other genres, although James Boswell's
biography of Samuel Johnson did draw attention to biographical
writing. The late 18th century saw a move towards Romanticism in
poetry in the *Lyrical Ballads* of Wordsworth and Coleridge.
Challenging the traditional strictness of both form and subject

matter, they used a much freer verse structure and drew their inspirations from the life and language of the rural class and the powers of the imagination. In Scotland, Robert Burns gave a distinctive voice to the rural population, addressing social issues as well as composing romantic verses.

1700

✝ DEATHS   John Dryden: English poet.

1701

✝ DEATHS   James VII and II: King of Scotland and England.

★ EVENTS   Act of Settlement: statute to determine the succession to the English throne after the death of Queen Anne. It excludes the Catholic Stuarts and states that all future monarchs must be members of the Church of England and may only leave the country with Parliamentary permission.

1702

✝ DEATHS   William III (William of Orange): King of England, Scotland and Ireland with Mary II. Dies following a fall from his horse.

★ EVENTS   War of the Spanish Succession (to 1713): nominally a war concerning the succession to the Spanish throne. However, the involvement of worldwide trade and colonial issues results in a war between England, the Holy Roman Empire and the United Provinces of the Netherlands against Spain and France. Alternatively known as Queen Anne's Wars.

1703

❀ BIRTHS   John Wesley: English evangelist and founder of Methodism.

✝ DEATHS   Samuel Pepys: English naval administrator and diarist. His diary gives a vivid picture of 17th-century life, especially of the Great Plague, the Great Fire of London and the arrival of the Dutch fleet.

1704

✝ DEATHS   John Locke: English empiricist philosopher, his
   sanctioning of revolution inspired both French and American
   revolutionaries. His most renowned work is the *Essay
   Concerning Human Understanding*.

★ EVENTS   (13 Aug) Battle of Blenheim: victory for England in
   alliance with Savoy against a Franco-Bavarian force. This is
   the first major English victory on the European mainland
   since Agincourt (1415).

1705

❀ BIRTHS   Dick Turpin: English robber and highwayman.

★ EVENTS   Building of Blenheim Palace (to 1724): a Baroque
   palace designed by Sir John Vanbrugh, built near Oxford.

1707

❀ BIRTHS   Henry Fielding: English playwright and novelist.

★ EVENTS   Union of the Parliaments: Act of Union unites
   England and Scotland under the name of Great Britain.

1708

❀ BIRTHS   William Pitt, 'the Elder': English politician and orator.

1709

❀ BIRTHS   John Cleland: English novelist, author of *Fanny Hill*.
   Samuel Johnson: English lexicographer, critic and poet.

★ EVENTS   Barrier Treaty: agreed between the English and the
   Dutch, following a similar Dutch–Spanish treaty in 1679,
   giving the Dutch the right to garrison towns in the southern
   Netherlands against French encroachment.

1711

❀ BIRTHS   David Hume: Scottish philosopher and historian.

★ EVENTS   Foundation of Ascot racecourse on Ascot Heath,
   Berkshire at the request of Queen Anne.

1713

✿ BIRTHS   Laurence Sterne: Irish novelist.

Allan Ramsay: Scottish portrait painter.

✶ EVENTS   Peace of Utrecht establishes peace following the War of the Spanish Succession; Britain gains Minorca, Gibraltar and North American territory.

1714

✝ DEATHS   Anne, Queen of Great Britain and Ireland, daughter of James VII (of Scotland) and II (of England).

✶ EVENTS   Riot Act: legislation aimed at preserving public order. When 12 or more people are assembled and refuse to disperse, they are, after a reading of the act by a person in authority, considered guilty of a serious crime.

1715

✝ DEATHS   Thomas Savery: English engineer, builder of the first practical steam engine.

✶ EVENTS   First Jacobite rebellion in Scotland in support of the claim to the throne of James Francis Edward Stuart (the 'Old Pretender') against the House of Hanover (to 1716). The uprising begins in Braemar with the Earl of Mar proclaiming the 'Old Pretender' king.

(13 Nov) The Jacobites are defeated at Sheriffmuir, despite having a superior force. This failure signals the collapse of the uprising; the French and Spanish effectively withdraw their support, and the cause cannot be revived despite the arrival of James Francis Edward Stuart at Peterhead on 22 December 1715.

1716

✿ BIRTHS   James Lind: Scottish physician and pioneer of the prevention and cure of scurvy.

✶ EVENTS   Septennial Act: legislation repealing the Triennial Act of 1694. This act extends the life of a Parliament from three to seven years and eases the transition to political stability and Whig supremacy in the early years of Hanoverian monarchy.

1718

✤ BIRTHS   Thomas Chippendale: English cabinet-maker.

★ EVENTS   Quadruple alliance of Britain, Austria, France and Netherlands against Spain (to 1720).

1719

✟ DEATHS   John Flamsteed: English astronomer and first Astronomer Royal. Compiler of an immense number of observations used by Isaac Newton to calculate his theory of gravitation.

William Paterson: Scottish financier and founder of the Bank of England.

Joseph Addison: English poet and essayist.

1720

✤ BIRTHS   Charles Edward Stuart, the 'Young Pretender', son of James Francis Edward Stuart. Claimant to the British throne.

★ EVENTS   South Sea Bubble: financial crisis arising out of speculation mania generated by Parliament's approval of the South Sea Company's plan to take over 60 per cent of the National Debt. Many investors are ruined in the aftermath, but Robert Walpole's plan for stock transfer retrieves the situation and makes his reputation.

1722

✤ BIRTHS   Flora Macdonald: Scottish heroine.

1723

✤ BIRTHS   Sir Joshua Reynolds: English portrait painter.

Adam Smith: Scottish economist and philosopher, author of *An Inquiry into the Nature and Causes of the Wealth of Nations*, the first major work of political economy.

✟ DEATHS   Christopher Wren: English architect, designed the new St Paul's, the Royal Exchange and the Greenwich Observatory.

1724

✻ BIRTHS   John Michell: English geologist and astronomer.

1725

✭ EVENTS   Treaty of Hanover: alliance of Britain, France,
Prussia, Sweden, Denmark and Netherlands.

1726

✞ DEATHS   Sir John Vanbrugh: English playwright and baroque
architect. Designer of Castle Howard and Blenheim Palace.

1727

✻ BIRTHS   Thomas Gainsborough: English landscape and
portrait painter.

✞ DEATHS   George I: King of Great Britain and Ireland, great-
grandson of James I of England, first of the Hanoverian line.

Sir Isaac Newton: English scientist and mathematician.
Discoverer of 'fluxions', an early form of calculus, deviser of
the first reflecting telescope and developer of the first theory
of gravitation.

✭ EVENTS   War between England and France against Spain (to
1729).

1728

✻ BIRTHS   Robert Adam: Scottish architect.

James Cook: English navigator.

Joseph Black: Scottish chemist, discoverer of carbon dioxide and
pioneer of the ideas of latent and specific heat.

1729

✻ BIRTHS   Edmund Burke: British statesman and political
philosopher.

1730

✻ BIRTHS   Josiah Wedgwood: English potter.

1731

❀ BIRTHS   Henry Cavendish: English natural philosopher and chemist, discoverer of the gas now known as hydrogen and the fact that water results from the union of two gases.

✞ DEATHS   Daniel Defoe: English writer.

★ EVENTS   Downing Street becomes the official residence of the Prime Minister.

1732

❀ BIRTHS   Richard Arkwright: English inventor and industrialist. Inventor of the water-powered spinning frame (1767).

1733

❀ BIRTHS   Joseph Priestley: English clergyman and chemist.

★ EVENTS   Patenting of John Kay's flying shuttle, a crucial development in textile manufacture.

1734

✞ DEATHS   Rob Roy MacGregor: Scottish outlaw.

1735

❀ BIRTHS   Robert Raikes: English philanthropist and founder of the Sunday School movement.

1736

❀ BIRTHS   James Watt: Scottish engineer and inventor, designer of the steam locomotive.

1737

❀ BIRTHS   Thomas Paine: British–American political writer.

Joseph Nollekens: English neoclassical sculptor.

1738

❀ BIRTHS   George III, King of Great Britain and Ireland, son of Frederick Louis, Prince of Wales. Succeeds his grandfather, George II, to the throne.

1739

✝ DEATHS   Dick Turpin: English robber and highwayman. He is
   caught and hanged in York.

★ EVENTS   War of Jenkins' Ear between Britain and Spain.
   Merges into the larger War of the Austrian Succession. Its
   name comes from Captain Robert Jenkins, who claims to have
   had his ear cut off by Spanish coast guards in the Caribbean.

1740

❀ BIRTHS   James Boswell: Scottish man of letters and biographer
   of Samuel Johnson.

✝ DEATHS   Jethro Tull: English agriculturalist, inventor of the
   seed drill which plants seeds in a straight line.

1742

✝ DEATHS   Edmond Halley: English astronomer and
   mathematician. Calculations of the orbits of comets enabled
   him to correctly predict the return of a comet sighted in 1682,
   now named after him.

1743

★ EVENTS   (27 Jun) Battle of Dettingen, during the War of the
   Austrian Succession. The British forces are commanded by
   George II, the last time a British monarch commands an army
   in the field.

1744

✝ DEATHS   Alexander Pope: English satirical poet.

1745

✝ DEATHS   Jonathan Swift: Anglo-Irish clergyman and satirist.

   Robert Walpole: English statesman whose period in office is
   widely held to have increased the influence of the House of
   Commons. He was the first to be recognized as 'Prime
   Minister', although this title was not constitutionally endorsed
   at this time.

★ EVENTS   The Forty-Five Rebellion: second Jacobite rebellion
   aiming to restore the Catholic Stuarts to the throne and

depose the Hanoverians. Charles Edward Stuart arrives in Britain and proclaims his father King James III. Supported mainly by the Highland Clans, the rebellion meets with early success such as the victory at Prestonpans (21 Sep), but support falls off as they move into England, and the uprising is finally defeated in 1746. After the Forty-Five, the Hanoverians brutally and systematically crush the clan system in the Highlands.

1746

✦ EVENTS   (16 Apr) Battle of Culloden: final defeat of the Jacobites by the English.

1748

❀ BIRTHS   Jeremy Bentham: English philosopher, jurist and social reformer. Co-founder of University College, London.

1749

❀ BIRTHS   Edward Jenner: English physician, pioneer of vaccination.

1752

❀ BIRTHS   John Nash: English architect and city planner.

1753

❀ BIRTHS   (c.) William Bligh: English sailor.

Sir John Soane: English architect.

✦ EVENTS   British Museum: established when the government acquire the art collection and library of Sir Hans Sloane.

1754

❀ BIRTHS   Josiah Spode: English potter.

✝ DEATHS   Henry Fielding: English playwright and novelist, most famous for his novel *Tom Jones*.

✦ EVENTS   Albany Congress: a meeting in Albany, New York, of representatives from seven British colonies in North America at which Benjamin Franklin proposes his 'plan of union' to unite the separate American British colonies. The Albany

Plan of Union is rejected by the Colonial governments and the Crown. However, the plan serves as a model for the joint action of the mainland colonies in the American Revolution.

St Andrews Royal and Ancient Golf Club, St Andrews, Scotland, is founded.

1756

❀ BIRTHS   John Loudon McAdam: Scottish inventor and engineer.

Henry Raeburn: Scottish portrait painter.

★ EVENTS   Seven Years War (to 1763): caused by colonial rivalry between Britain and France.

Treaty of Westminster: alliance between Britain and Prussia.

Black Hole of Calcutta: the small room in which British defenders are held captive after the fall of Calcutta to the Nawab of Bengal. It is claimed that only 23 out of 146 prisoners survived. The incident is famed in the history of British colonialism but it seems likely that the facts have been exaggerated.

1757

❀ BIRTHS   William Blake: English poet, painter, engraver and mystic.

Thomas Telford: British engineer.

★ EVENTS   Treaty of Alinagar: concluded by Clive of Plassey following his recapture of Calcutta from the Nawab of Bengal. Under its terms, Calcutta is returned to the British East India Company, its privileges are renewed and the rights to fortify the town and mint money are secured. This provides a bridgehead from which to increase the Company's power in Bengal.

1758

❀ BIRTHS   Viscount Horatio Nelson: British admiral.

✝ DEATHS   Allan Ramsay: Scottish poet.

★ EVENTS   The world's first railway line is opened in Leeds.

1759

❀ BIRTHS   William Wilberforce: English politician, evangelist and philanthropist.

William Pitt, 'the Younger': English politician.

Mary Wollstonecraft: Anglo-Irish writer and pioneer of women's rights. Author of *Vindication of the Rights of Woman*.

Robert Burns: Scottish poet.

✭ EVENTS   (13 Sep) Battle of Quebec: battle fought during the Seven Years War between the British and French forces defending Quebec. It follows a daring plan to transport British troops from the St Lawrence River up steep, wooded cliffs. British victory leads to speedy capture of Quebec and the subsequent collapse of French power in Canada.

The Caron Iron Company on the west coast of Scotland pioneer the smelting of iron using coke.

1760

❀ BIRTHS   Thomas Clarkson: English philanthropist, crusader against African slavery.

✝ DEATHS   George II: King of Great Britain and Ireland, son of George I. Succeeded by his grandson, George III.

1761

✝ DEATHS   Samuel Richardson: English novelist, most famous for his novel *Clarissa*.

1762

❀ BIRTHS   George IV: King of Great Britain and Hanover, son of George III.

✭ EVENTS   Britain declares war on Spain.

1763

❀ BIRTHS   William Cobbett: English journalist and reformer.

✭ EVENTS   Treaty of Paris: treaty ends the Seven Years War. In the short term, Britain is isolated by the French determination for revenge, but the final consequence is British colonial supremacy. France accepts final defeat in the French and

Indian War, the last of the 18th-century wars between France and Britain for the control of North America.

1764

❀ BIRTHS   Charles Grey: British politician and Prime Minister.

✯ EVENTS   Sugar Act: British statute that attempts for the first time to raise colonial revenue without reference to the colonial assemblies. Its main aim is to impose and collect customs duties and to prevent illegal trade. The colonials respond with protest, but the act is sporadically enforced until the complete breakdown of British–American relations.

1765

❀ BIRTHS   William IV: King of Great Britain and Ireland, and King of Hanover, son of George III.

✯ EVENTS   Stamp Act: a British act which levies a direct tax on all papers required in discharging official business in the American colonies. It is the first direct tax levied without the consent of the colonial assemblies, and it causes much discontent in the colonies, six of which petition against it.

The Isle of Man is partly purchased by the British government (wholly in 1828).

1766

❀ BIRTHS   Thomas Robert Malthus: English economist.

John Dalton: English chemist and natural philosopher.

♱ DEATHS   James Francis Edward Stuart, the 'Old Pretender', son of James VII and II. Dies in Rome.

✯ EVENTS   Declaratory Act: after much opposition in the US colonies to the introduction of taxes by the preceding administration, the Stamp Act (1765) is repealed. However, the Declaratory Act reasserts the British parliament's general right to legislate for the colonies 'in all cases whatsoever'.

1767

✯ EVENTS   Townshend Acts: British statutes imposing taxes on five categories of goods imported into the American colonies,

after successful colonial resistance to the Stamp Act (1765).
The Townshend Taxes likewise meet resistance from the
colonists, and four categories are repealed in 1770. The fifth,
on tea, remains in effect until the Boston Tea Party (1773).
The acts are named after British Chancellor of the Exchequer,
Charles Townshend, who sponsors them.

1768

✿ **BIRTHS**   Sir Astley Cooper: English surgeon.

♱ **DEATHS**   Laurence Sterne: Irish novelist, best known for his
novel *The Life and Opinions of Tristram Shandy*. Dies of
pleurisy.

✭ **EVENTS**   Royal Academy of Arts: a British academy founded
under royal patronage, aiming to hold annual exhibitions
(still held) to raise the status of artists, and to foster the
development of a national school of painting to rival the
schools of the continent. Sir Joshua Reynolds is its first
president.

Captain James Cook sets sail in the *Endeavour* from Whitby,
England, bound for Tahiti.

1769

✿ **BIRTHS**   Duke of Wellington: Irish-born British general and
politician. Will later defeat Napoleon I at the Battle of
Waterloo.

Robert Stewart Castlereagh: British politician.

1770

✿ **BIRTHS**   George Canning: English politician.

James Hogg: Scottish poet and novelist.

William Wordsworth: English poet.

Earl of Liverpool: English politician.

✭ **EVENTS**   (5 Mar) Boston Massacre: the first bloodshed of the
American Revolution. In an atmosphere of intense
resentment against British troops and regulations, British
guards open fire on an unruly crowd, killing five. Of the nine
British soldiers tried for murder, seven, including the

commander, are acquitted and two are found guilty of
manslaughter.

1771

✿ BIRTHS   Robert Owen: Welsh social reformer.

Sir Walter Scott: Scottish poet and novelist.

1772

✿ BIRTHS   Samuel Taylor Coleridge: English poet.

★ EVENTS   Mansfield Judgement: in a case involving a runaway
black slave, the name given to the ruling by Lord Justice
Mansfield that slavery is neither allowed nor approved under
English law. It effectively abolishes slavery in England and
Wales.

1773

✿ BIRTHS   Henry 'Orator' Hunt: English radical agitator.

★ EVENTS   India Acts: passed by the British parliament,
encompass the Regulating Act of 1773 and India Act of 1784
which attempt to reform the corrupt and inefficient
administration of the British East India Company over the
developing Indian empire. The 1773 Act sets up the post of
Governor-General and a Governing Council in India and that
of 1784 establishes a Board of Control in London.

Boston Tea Party: in the events leading up to the American
Revolution, the climactic act of resistance to British attempts
at direct taxation. It results in the destruction of 342 chests of
dutied tea by working men disguised as Indians. Other ports
had refused to let the tea ships enter.

1774

✿ BIRTHS   Sir Charles Bell: Scottish anatomist, surgeon and
neurophysiological pioneer.

★ EVENTS   Intolerable Acts: the American name for laws passed
by parliament in London to punish Massachusetts for the
Boston Tea Party. They are the Boston Port Act, the
Massachusetts Government Act, the Administration of
Justice Act, and a Quartering Act. The Quebec Act, though

addressing a different problem (that of colonial rule as opposed to the French seigniorial system) is also taken by colonists to add insult to the injury of the Intolerable Acts.

1775

✿ BIRTHS   Jane Austen: English novelist.

Daniel O'Connell: Irish political leader, founder of the Repeal Association to agitate for an end to Irish union with Britain.

Joseph Mallord William Turner: English landscape artist and watercolourist.

James Parkinson: English physician: discoverer of Parkinson's disease and appendicitis.

★ EVENTS   American Revolution: beginning of the war that establishes the 13 American colonies as independent from Britain, often called the American War of Independence. Britain takes measures to tighten control over the colonies and the situation comes to a head over the issue of Parliament's right to tax the colonies without their representation.

(17 Jun) Battle of Bunker Hill: the first pitched battle of the American Revolution, technically an American defeat. The British garrison dislodges New England troops from their position overlooking occupied Boston, but very high British casualties demonstrate American fighting ability, and discourage attempts on other American emplacements.

(19 Apr) Battles of Lexington and Concord: fought in Massachusetts after British troops try to seize supplies stored at the village of Concord, and are confronted by colonial militia. Results in British defeat.

1776

✿ BIRTHS   John Constable: English landscape painter.

♱ DEATHS   David Hume: Scottish philosopher and historian, best known for *A Treatise on Human Nature*.

★ EVENTS   Declaration of Independence: the document adopted by the US Continental Congress to proclaim the separation of the 13 colonies from Britain. Drawn up by a committee of John Adams, Benjamin Franklin, Thomas Jefferson, Robert R. Livingston, and Roger Sherman, it announces the right of

revolution, details the Americans' reasons for the break, and
asserts that American government should be based on a theory
of natural law, and should respect the fundamental rights of
individuals.

1777

★ EVENTS   (11 Sep) Battle of Brandywine Creek: British troops
defeat an American force under George Washington, but
subsequently fail to consolidate the success.

(19 Sep–17 Oct) Battles of Saratoga: among the most important
engagements of the American Revolution. Actually fought
near modern Schuylerville, New York, the battles result in the
defeat of a large British army by American continental troops
and militia. The outcome ends British plans to cut New
England off from the rest of the states, and encourages French
intervention on the American side.

1778

❀ BIRTHS   William Hazlitt: English essayist.

✝ DEATHS   William Pitt 'the Elder': English politician and orator.
Dies during a debate in Parliament.

1779

❀ BIRTHS   Richard Oastler: English social reformer, campaigner
on behalf of the poor to improve their living and working
conditions.

✝ DEATHS   James Cook: English navigator. After travelling to
Tahiti, Australia, New Zealand, Hawaii, Canada and the
Antarctic, he is killed by natives in Hawaii.

Thomas Chippendale: English cabinet-maker, famous for his
elegant neoclassical furniture, especially chairs.

1780

❀ BIRTHS   Thomas Chalmers: Scottish theologian and reformer,
leader of the 1843 Disruption.

★ EVENTS   The Gordon Riots: anti-Catholic riots in London
which cause a breakdown of law and order in parts of the
capital for several days. They occur after Lord George

Gordon, leader of the Protestant Association, fails in his attempt to have clauses in the 1778 Catholic Relief Act (removing restrictions on the activities of priests) repealed.

(16 Aug) Battle of Camden: a battle of the American Revolution, fought in South Carolina. After the British capture of Charleston, Camden is the first major battle of the southern campaign. Results in American defeat.

(11 Feb–12 May) Battles of Charleston: during the American Revolution, the victorious British siege of Charleston, South Carolina, which marks the beginning of the southern phase of British strategy. At a small cost, British troops capture a 5,400-strong American garrison and a squadron of four ships.

Establishment of Sunday School by Robert Raikes where deprived and uneducated children may learn to read and repeat the Catechism; similar schools soon spread throughout England.

1781

❀ BIRTHS   George Stephenson: British inventor, designer of the locomotive and builder of the '*Rocket*', his most famous engine.

✯ EVENTS   (17 Jan) Battle of Cowpens: during the American Revolution, an engagement in South Carolina resulting in American victory.

(30 Aug–19 Oct) Yorktown Campaign: the final major campaign of the American Revolution, in which the British Army is trapped at Yorktown in Virginia, by troops under George Washington and a French fleet. The defeat destroys the political will on the British side to continue the war. It causes the fall of Lord North, Prime Minister since 1770, and opens the way for peace negotiations.

1782

✯ EVENTS   (12 Apr) Battle of the Saintes: a major Caribbean Anglo-French naval action during the American Revolution. In that war, France and Spain have sided with Britain's rebellious North American colonists and used the British preoccupation with the Americans to obtain naval supremacy and capture British colonies in the Caribbean. In 1782 the British admiral George Rodney returns from Europe to shadow the French commander who is planning to attack Jamaica. Battle is joined off the Saintes (the small rocky islets between Dominica and Guadeloupe) and, after a day of heavy fighting, Britain is victorious. Rodney is hailed as the saviour of Jamaica.

1784

❀ BIRTHS   Lord Palmerston: English statesman.

Earl of Aberdeen: Scottish politician and Prime Minster of Britain.

✝ DEATHS   Samuel Johnson: English lexicographer, critic and poet.

Allan Ramsay: Scottish portrait painter, appointed portrait painter to George III in 1767.

★ EVENTS   Founding of New Lanark, a mill village in Scotland; it becomes the setting for the experimental social ideas of Robert Owen.

1785

❀ BIRTHS   Sir David Wilkie: Scottish painter.

★ EVENTS   Foundation of the *Daily Universal Register*, the British daily newspaper renamed *The Times* in 1788.

Edmund Cartwright invents the power loom for weaving.

1786

❀ BIRTHS   Sir John Franklin: English Arctic explorer. He will be credited with the discovery of the Northwest Passage.

1787

★ EVENTS   Foundation of the Society for the Effecting of the Abolition of the Slave Trade, otherwise known as the Anti-Slavery Society.

1788

❀ BIRTHS   George Byron: English poet.

Sir Robert Peel: English politician.

✝ DEATHS   Thomas Gainsborough: English landscape and portrait painter, one of the great English masters and founder of the English School.

Charles Edward Stuart, the 'Young Pretender', son of James Francis Edward Stuart. Dies in Rome.

1789

✿ BIRTHS   John Martin: English painter.

✝ DEATHS   John Cleland: English novelist, author of *Fanny Hill*, which was labelled obscene as late as 1963.

1790

✝ DEATHS   Flora Macdonald: Scottish heroine. Conducted Charles Edward Stuart to safety in Skye after the failure of the Forty-Five Rebellion.

Adam Smith: Scottish economist and philosopher, author of *An Inquiry into the Nature and Causes of the Wealth of Nations*, the first major work of political economy.

1791

✿ BIRTHS   Michael Faraday: English chemist and physicist.

✝ DEATHS   John Wesley: English evangelist and founder of methodism.

★ EVENTS   Foundation of the Society of United Irishmen, a society formed in Belfast in 1791 by Protestant lawyer Wolfe Tone. It supports the French Revolution and espouses both religious equality and parliamentary reform. As agitation increases, so United Irishmen become increasingly associated with support for Catholicism. The society raises French support for the unsuccessful Irish rebellion of 1798, and afterwards goes into decline.

1792

✿ BIRTHS   Charles Babbage: English mathematician, pioneer of calculating machines and the computer.

Percy Bysshe Shelley: English Romantic poet.

✝ **DEATHS**   Robert Adam: Scottish architect. He transformed the prevailing Palladian fashion in architecture by using a series of romantically elegant variations on Classical originals.

Sir Richard Arkwright: English inventor of the water-powered spinning frame (1767).

Sir Joshua Reynolds: English portrait painter, who became first President of the Royal Academy in 1768.

1793

✝ **DEATHS**   John Michell: English geologist and astronomer, best known as the founder of seismology.

★ **EVENTS**   Revolutionary France declares war on Britain, Spain and the Dutch Republic.

1794

❀ **BIRTHS**   Feargus O'Connor: Irish Chartist leader.

✝ **DEATHS**   James Lind: Scottish physician and pioneer of the prevention and cure of scurvy.

★ **EVENTS**   (1 Jun) Battle of the Glorious First of June: a naval battle fought off the Isle d'Ouessant (near Brest) between British and French navies. Victory for the British results in the capture of a third of the French ships, and confirmation of British naval supremacy.

Jay's Treaty: an agreement between the USA and Britain to end the British occupation of military posts in the northwestern parts of US territory, and to alter the terms of US commerce with Britain and its colonies. Negotiated by John Jay, it is very unpopular with the US public, largely because of the restrictions it imposes on US trade with the West Indies.

1795

❀ **BIRTHS**   John Keats: English poet.

Thomas Carlyle: Scottish historian and man of letters.

✝ **DEATHS**   James Boswell: Scottish man of letters and biographer of Samuel Johnson.

Josiah Wedgwood: English potter.

★ EVENTS   Establishment of the Orange Society, an association
  that develops into the Orange Order. Aims to counteract
  growing Catholic influence in Ireland and 'to maintain the
  laws and peace of the country and the Protestant
  constitution'. The name is taken from the Protestant Dutch
  dynasty represented by William III of Orange. Organized in
  'Lodges', it provides the backbone of resistance to Home Rule
  proposals.

  Speenhamland system: the most famous of many local
  expedients to improve the operation of the old Poor Laws at
  a time of crisis. The name is taken from the Berkshire parish
  whose magistrates in 1795 introduce scales of relief for
  labourers dependent both on the prevailing price of bread and
  the size of labourers' families. The principles spread to many
  southern and eastern parishes in the early 19th century. It is
  much criticized by political economists for encouraging the
  poor to breed.

1796

✝ DEATHS   Robert Burns: Scottish poet.

1797

❀ BIRTHS   Mary Shelley: English writer, best known for her novel
  Frankenstein.

✝ DEATHS   Mary Wollstonecraft: Anglo-Irish author and pioneer
  of women's rights. Author of *Vindication of the Rights of
  Woman*. Dies giving birth to her daughter, later Mary Shelley.

  Edmund Burke: British statesman and political philosopher,
  best known for his work *Reflections on the French Revolution*.

★ EVENTS   (14 Feb) Battle of Cape St Vincent: British navy
  defeats numerically superior Franco-Spanish fleet, thus
  preventing French plans for the assembly of a combined
  invasion fleet to conquer Britain.

  (11 Oct) Battle of Camperdown: a naval battle between British
  and Dutch fleets off Texel Island, Holland. The British
  virtually destroy the Dutch Fleet, frustrating its attempt to
  disable the British North Sea squadron and thus facilitate the
  invasion of Britain.

1798

★ EVENTS   Unsuccessful rebellion at Vinegar Hill, Ireland, by
    United Irishmen.

   (1 Aug) Battle of Aboukir Bay: a naval battle during the War of
    the Second Coalition, in which the British Admiral Nelson
    destroys the French fleet off the coast of Egypt; the
    engagement is also known as the Battle of the Nile. This victory
    forces Napoleon I to abandon his Egyptian campaign, aimed
    at threatening British territory in India, and return to France.

1799

☦ DEATHS   Joseph Black: Scottish chemist, discoverer of carbon
    dioxide and pioneer of the ideas of latent and specific heat.

★ EVENTS   Coalition of Britain, Austria, Russia, Portugal,
    Naples and Ottoman Empire against France.

   Combination Acts: British legislation which prohibits the
    coming together ('combination') of workers in trade unions.
    The Acts are part of anti-reformist legislation passed by the
    Pitt government during the French wars, though
    combinations in many trades are already illegal.

19th Century

The 19th century in Britain was dominated by the reign of Queen Victoria. Technological progress brought further changes in industry and with it, political unrest. The Chartist movement agitated for parliamentary reform, and the vote was gradually extended as the century wore on, to include middle-class men (1832) and male settled tenants in boroughs (1867) and in rural and mining areas (1884). Religious reform occurred with the Disruption of the Church of Scotland, and the publication of Charles Darwin's *Origin of Species* introduced the idea of evolution, which conflicted with much religious thinking about the creation of the universe.

Literature in the early 19th century was split between the influences of the young Romantic poets, such as Keats, Shelley and Byron, and novelists like Jane Austen and George Eliot who wrote about the more mundane realities of life. The mid- to late 1900s produced some of the most popular British writers — Walter Scott, Robert Louis Stevenson, the Brontë sisters, Charles Dickens, Thomas Hardy and Anthony Trollope.

In art, the work of Constable and Turner proved unpopular with the Pre-Raphaelite Brotherhood, active from the mid-1800s, who aimed to revitalize British art by reverting to the simplicity and freshness of Italian art before Raphael. The principal artists of this movement were John Everett Millais and Dante Gabriel Rossetti.

Architecture and design were influenced by the Gothic revival and Art Nouveau. Scottish architect Charles Rennie Mackintosh brought the potential of Art Nouveau to the attention of Europe. The Gothic-inspired work of August Pugin, who was responsible for much of the decoration and sculpture for the Houses of Parliament, was also especially influential. With William Morris he developed the Arts and Crafts Movement which strove to revive craftsmanship in the face of late 19th-century mass production.

Photography was pioneered by William Fox Talbot, and by the

middle of the century David Octavius Hill was using the Calotype process to produce the first artistic photographic portraits.

Music in the 19th century spawned the composers Delius, Holst and Elgar, as well as the light operatic works of Gilbert and Sullivan.

1800

✿ BIRTHS   William Henry Fox Talbot: English pioneer of photography.

1801

✿ BIRTHS   Anthony Shaftesbury: British factory reformer and philanthropist.

★ EVENTS   Act of Union unites Great Britain and Ireland to form the United Kingdom.

1802

✿ BIRTHS   Sir Edwin Landseer: English artist.

★ EVENTS   Treaty of Amiens: a treaty between Britain and France, marking the end of the first stage of the wars with revolutionary France. It is agreed that most of the land conquered by either power since 1793 is to be returned. However, war breaks out afresh in 1803, continuing until 1815.

Factory Acts: legislation passed to regulate employment in factories. The early acts generally concentrate on limiting the working hours of women and children in textile factories only.

Founding of Ampleforth College, Yorkshire.

1803

★ EVENTS   Thomas Telford begins construction of the Caledonian Canal, Scotland (completed 1823).

1804

✿ BIRTHS   Benjamin Disraeli: British politician and Prime Minister.

Richard Cobden: English economist and politician, known as

the Apostle of Free Trade. Founding member of the Anti-Corn Law League.

✝ DEATHS   Joseph Priestley: English clergyman and chemist, identifier of the gas later named oxygen by Lavoisier.

1805

✾ BIRTHS   Sir William Hamilton: Irish mathematician whose studies will be the forerunner of much modern algebra.

✝ DEATHS   Viscount Horatio Nelson: British admiral. Dies after being mortally wounded at the Battle of Trafalgar.

✭ EVENTS   (21 Oct) Battle of Trafalgar: the most famous naval engagement of the Napoleonic Wars, which destroys Napoleon I's hopes of invading England and establishes British naval supremacy for a century. Fought off Cape Trafalgar, Spain, between the British and Franco-Spanish fleets; the British triumph is marred by the death of Nelson at the moment of victory.

War of the Grand Alliance (to 1807): part of the Napoleonic Wars. A coalition of Britain, Austria, Russia, Prussia and Sweden is formed to attack France from the sea. The coalition is undermined by spectacular French victories.

1806

✾ BIRTHS   John Stuart Mill: English philosopher and utilitarian reformer, supporter of female suffrage and liberalism.

Isambard Kingdom Brunel: English engineer and inventor.

✝ DEATHS   William Pitt, the 'Younger': English politician. Heavy drinking contributes to his early death while still in office.

1807

✭ EVENTS   Slave trade abolished in British Empire. The Society for the Effecting of the Abolition of the Slave Trade was founded in 1787. It is spearheaded by the 'Clapham Sect' or 'Saints', who find a political voice in William Wilberforce, the MP for Yorkshire. Although Wilberforce's abolition bill lacks government support during the Pitt administration, in 1806 the Tories are replaced by the Whigs and the bill becomes law a year later. The last British slave trader, the *Kitty Amelia,* leaves Liverpool in May 1808.

Treaty of Tilsit: ends the War of the Grand Alliance.

1808

❀ BIRTHS   Thomas Cook: British railway excursion and tourist pioneer.

★ EVENTS   Peninsular War (to 1814): the prolonged struggle for the Iberian Peninsula between the occupying French and a British army under Wellington supported by Portuguese and Spanish forces. Known in Spain as the 'War of Independence' and to Napoleonic France as 'the Spanish ulcer', it starts as a Spanish revolt against the imposition of Napoleon I's brother as King of Spain, but develops into a bitter conflict. Following Napoleon's Moscow campaign (1812), French resources are over-extended, enabling Wellington's army to invade south-west France.

1809

❀ BIRTHS   William Ewart Gladstone: English politician and Prime Minister.

Charles Darwin: English naturalist, whose great work will be *The Origin of Species by Means of Natural Selection* (1859).

Alfred, Lord Tennyson: English poet.

✟ DEATHS   Thomas Paine: British-American political writer. Author of *The Rights of Man* which upholds the ideas of the French Revolution.

1810

✟ DEATHS   Henry Cavendish: English natural philosopher and chemist, discoverer of the gas now known as hydrogen and the fact that water results from the union of two gases.

1811

❀ BIRTHS   John Bright: British politician and leading member of the Anti-Corn Law League.

Sir James Young Simpson: Scottish obstetrician, pioneer of chloroform as an anaesthetic.

William Makepeace Thackeray: English novelist.

Sir George Gilbert Scott: English architect.

✝ DEATHS   Robert Raikes: English philanthropist and founder of the Sunday School movement.

✸ EVENTS   Regency under the Prince of Wales (to 1820).

Luddites (to 1812): the name given to the group of workers who destroy newly-introduced textile machinery in Nottingham, Yorkshire and Lancashire. Their fear is that the output of the equipment is so much faster than the output of a hand-loom operator that many jobs will be lost. Known as 'the Luds', after their leader, Ned Ludd. When the movement ends with a mass trial in York in 1813 many are hanged or transported to Australia. The term has since been used to describe any resistance to technological innovation.

Founding of Charterhouse School, Surrey.

1812

✽ BIRTHS   Robert Browning: English poet.

Charles Dickens: English novelist.

Augustus Pugin: English architect.

✸ EVENTS   War of 1812: the name given to the hostilities between Britain and the United States between 1812 and 1814. Its deepest causes go back to some unfulfilled provisions of the Peace of 1783, which secured American independence. However, war is eventually provoked by the persistent refusal of Britain to recognize American maritime rights. The USA eventually has no other option but to declare war in order to protect her independence. The British are militarily more effective, gaining victory with their Indian allies against American attempts to gain Canadian land, and even burning down the Capitol and the White House in Washington.

1813

✽ BIRTHS   David Livingstone: Scottish missionary and explorer.

John Snow: English anaesthetist and epidemiologist, identifier of the link between cholera and contaminated water supplies.

1814

★ EVENTS   Treaty of Ghent: the treaty between the USA and
Britain which ends the War of 1812. Marks a change in
Britain's attitude to the USA and allows a mutually beneficial
commercial relationship to develop. However, the issues from
which the war initially grew — maritime and military control
of the Great Lakes — are not fully resolved.

1815

❀ BIRTHS   Anthony Trollope: English novelist.

★ EVENTS   (18 Jun) Battle of Waterloo: the final defeat of
Napoleon I by the Duke of Wellington, ending the Napoleonic
Wars and the Emperor's last bid for power in the Hundred
Days. It is a hard-fought battle in which a number of crucial
blunders by the French contribute to their defeat.

Treaties of Paris (1814–15): peace settlements involving France
and the victorious coalition of Britain, Austria, Prussia,
Russia, Sweden and Portugal, restoring the Bourbon
monarchy to France in place of the Napoleonic Empire. In
1815 a large indemnity and army of occupation replaced the
generous terms of 1814.

Introduction of the Corn Laws: legislation regulating the trade
in corn. Inspired by rapidly dropping market prices, it
imposes prohibitively high duties on the import of foreign
corn when the domestic price is lower than 80 shillings a
quarter. Widely criticized by radical politicians as legislation
designed to protect the landed interest at the expense of the
ordinary consumer.

Holy Alliance: the alliance concluded after the final defeat of
Napoleon I between Austria, Britain, Prussia and Russia. It
is designed to ensure the exclusion of the House of Bonaparte
from power in France and to guarantee the monarchist order
in Europe. Each power makes specific military commitments
in the event of war with France. Despite this, royalist France
itself joins the alliance at the Congress of Aachen (Aix-la-
Chapelle) in 1818.

1816

✿ BIRTHS   Charlotte Brontë: English novelist.

1817

✝ DEATHS   William Bligh: English sailor. Commander of the
Bounty when the crew mutinied (1789). Cast adrift without
charts he arrived in Java having travelled 3,618 miles in an
open boat. Later became governor of New South Wales
(1805) and was promoted to the Admiralty.

Jane Austen: English novelist.

★ EVENTS   Rush–Bagot Convention: an agreement between the
USA and Britain to demilitarize the Great Lakes by limiting
the number, tonnage, and armament of ships on each side.
The convention ends the threat of a Great Lakes arms race,
but complete disarmament on the US–Canada border does
not follow until decades later.

1818

✿ BIRTHS   Emily Brontë: English novelist and poet.

★ EVENTS   Founding of Dollar Academy, Clackmannanshire.

1819

✿ BIRTHS   Victoria: Queen of Great Britain and Empress of
India, daughter of Edward, Duke of Kent.

Albert, Prince consort of Queen Victoria.

George Eliot (pseudonym of Mary Ann or Marian Evans):
English novelist.

John Ruskin: English writer and art critic.

✝ DEATHS   James Watt: Scottish engineer and inventor, designer
of the steam locomotive.

★ EVENTS   Peterloo Massacre at Manchester: popular meeting
about parliamentary reform is violently dispersed by the
Manchester Yeomanry; 11 people are killed.

1820

✿ BIRTHS   Anne Brontë: English novelist and poet.

Florence Nightingale: British hospital reformer.

✝ DEATHS   George III, King of Great Britain and Ireland, son of
      Frederick Louis, Prince of Wales. Succeeded his grandfather,
      George II to the throne. Mentally ill from 1810, he dies insane
      and blind.

✯ EVENTS   Cato Street Conspiracy: a plot formulated by Arthur
      Thistlewood and fellow radical conspirators to blow up the
      British Tory Cabinet during a dinner at the Earl of Harrowby's
      house. The plot is infiltrated by a government agent, and the
      leaders are arrested and hanged.

1821

✝ DEATHS   John Keats: English poet. Dies in Rome of
      tuberculosis.

1822

✝ DEATHS   Robert Stewart Castlereagh: British politician.
      Commits suicide under the belief that he is being blackmailed
      for homosexuality.

   Percy Bysshe Shelley: English Romantic poet. Drowns in a
      boating accident near Leghorn, Italy.

1823

✝ DEATHS   Joseph Nollekens: English neoclassical sculptor.

   Edward Jenner: English physician, pioneer of vaccination.

   Henry Raeburn: Scottish portrait painter.

✯ EVENTS   The construction of the Caledonian Canal, Scotland
      (begun 1803), is completed by Thomas Telford.

1824

❀ BIRTHS   William Thomson Kelvin: British natural
      philosopher.

✝ DEATHS   George Byron: English poet. Dies of marsh fever
      while fighting with the Greeks against the Turks.

   James Parkinson: English physician, discoverer of Parkinson's
      disease and appendicitis.

✯ EVENTS   Anglo-Burmese Wars (1824–6, 1852–3 and 1885):
      three wars which secure British control of Burma.

Opening of the National Gallery, London: houses the largest collection of paintings in Britain.

1825

✯ EVENTS   Rebuilding of Buckingham Palace by John Nash for George IV. The palace, however, remains unused until Queen Victoria's accession in 1837.

The first passenger railway is opened, running between Stockton and Darlington.

1827

❀ BIRTHS   Frances Mary Buss: English pioneer of higher education for women.

Joseph Lister: English surgeon, pioneer of the antiseptic system which revolutionizes modern surgery.

✝ DEATHS   George Canning: English politician.

William Blake: English poet, painter, engraver and mystic.

Josiah Spode: English potter. He was appointed potter to George III in 1806.

✯ EVENTS   (20 Oct) Battle of Navarino Bay: a battle fought when the British and French (with the agreement of the Russians) destroy the Turkish and Egyptian fleets off south-west Greece. The outcome is an important factor in the achievement of Greek independence from the Ottoman Empire, which is formally recognized in 1828.

1828

❀ BIRTHS   Dante Gabriel Rossetti: English poet and painter, co-founder of the Pre-Raphaelite Brotherhood.

✝ DEATHS   Earl of Liverpool: English politician. Dies following a fit of apoplexy.

✯ EVENTS   Repeal of the Test Act. The act is originally passed to curb Catholic influence at the court of Charles II. Every office holder has to take Oaths of Supremacy and Allegiance, and to take communion according to the rites of the Church of England.

The Iron industry is revolutionized by the introduction of the hot-blast method of production. This reduces the amount of fuel consumed in the process, cuts the cost of production and allows the exploitation of blackband ironstone, found uniquely in Scotland.

1829

❀ BIRTHS Sir John Everett Millais: English painter, co-founder of the Pre-Raphaelite Brotherhood.

★ EVENTS Building of George Stephenson's '*Rocket*'.

Catholic Emancipation: a reluctant religious concession granted by the Tory government, headed by the Duke of Wellington, following mounting agitation in Ireland led by Daniel O'Connell and the Catholic Association. Roman Catholics are permitted to become MPs; all offices of state in Ireland, except Viceroy and Chancellor, are also opened to Catholics.

1830

❀ BIRTHS Robert Cecil: English politician and Prime Minister of Great Britain.

✝ DEATHS George IV: King of the United Kingdom and Hanover, son of George III. Prince Regent from 1810 owing to his father's insanity.

William Hazlitt, English essayist.

★ EVENTS Gibraltar becomes a British Crown Colony.

1832

❀ BIRTHS Lewis Carroll (pseudonym of Charles Lutwidge Dodgson): English writer.

✝ DEATHS Sir Walter Scott: Scottish poet and novelist.

Jeremy Bentham: English philosopher, jurist and social reformer. Co-founder of University College, London.

★ EVENTS First Reform Act: legislation in Britain which alters parliamentary constituencies and increases the size of the electorate. Enfranchises almost all middle class men and creates 42 new English boroughs.

1833

✿ BIRTHS   Sir Edward Burne-Jones: English painter and designer.

✝ DEATHS   William Wilberforce: English politician, evangelist and philanthropist. Founder of the movement which resulted in the abolition of slavery in the British West Indies.

✰ EVENTS   Factory Act: prohibits children under nine from working in textile mills, and appoints the first factory inspectors. Legislation for a maximum 10-hour working day for women and older children is introduced in 1847.

Emancipation Acts: statutes of imperial legislatures which free colonial slaves. They grant financial compensation to the slave owners and free the slaves under a system of apprenticeship on 1 August 1834. On that date 750,000 slaves become free in the British West Indies.

1834

✿ BIRTHS   William Morris: English craftsman and poet.

✝ DEATHS   Thomas Telford: British engineer, best known for his work on bridges and canals.

Thomas Robert Malthus: English economist, his *Essay on the Principle of Population* argued that the population has a natural tendency to increase faster than the means of subsistence, and that efforts should be made to cut the birth rate — a view later known as Malthusianism. Pioneer of the idea of the Malthusian Check, arguing that natural disasters such as flood, famine and earthquake are necessary curbs on population growth.

Samuel Taylor Coleridge: English poet.

✰ EVENTS   Tolpuddle Martyrs: a group of agricultural labourers are transported after being convicted of taking illegal oaths and organising into a Trade Union.

1835

✝ DEATHS   William Cobbett: English journalist and reformer.

James Hogg: Scottish poet and novelist.

John Nash: English architect and city planner. Planner of the layout of the new Regent's Park (1811–25). He also redesigned and was architect of Buckingham Palace and the Marble Arch which stood in front of it. He laid out Trafalgar Square and St James's Park, and rebuilt the Royal Pavilion, Brighton, in Oriental style.

Henry 'Orator' Hunt: English radical agitator, who advocated the repeal of the Corn Laws, parliamentary reform and democracy.

1836

❀ BIRTHS   Sir Henry Campbell-Bannerman: Scottish politician and Prime Minister of Britain.

Elizabeth Garrett Anderson: British physician, pioneer for the admission of women into medicine and first woman mayor in England.

W S Gilbert: English parodist and librettist of the 'Gilbert and Sullivan' light operas, in partnership with Sir Arthur Sullivan.

✝ DEATHS   John Loudon McAdam: Scottish inventor and engineer. Inventor of the 'macadamized' road using crushed stone bound in gravel, raised to improve drainage.

1837

✝ DEATHS   William IV: King of Great Britain and Ireland, and King of Hanover, son of George III. Last monarch to use prerogative powers to dismiss a ministry with a parliamentary majority.

Sir John Soane: English architect. His designs include the Bank of England and Dulwich College Art Gallery.

John Constable: English landscape painter.

1838

❀ BIRTHS   Octavia Hill: English housing reformer and founder of the National Trust.

★ EVENTS   Chartist Movement: develops in support of democratic political reform, and remains active to 1849. Its name derives from the 'People's Charter' presented twice to parliament (1839 and 1842) which calls for universal manhood suffrage, voting by secret ballot, the abolition of property qualifications for MPs, payment for MPs, equally-sized constituencies and annually elected parliaments. All but the last of these are obtained, but the movement, largely of working people, threatens and occasionally alarms the authorities, who arrest and imprison its leaders during the main phase of the agitation.

Anti-Corn Law League: an association formed in Manchester, largely under the patronage of businessmen and industrialists, to repeal the British Corn Laws, which impose protective tariffs on the import of foreign corn. League propaganda aids the growing movement for free trade in early 19th-century Britain, and the league is an influential political pressure group with many supporters in parliament.

Relocation of the National Gallery from Pall Mall to Trafalgar Square.

(c.) Iron production in Scotland is cheaper than anywhere else in great Britain.

1839

❀ BIRTHS George Cadbury: English businessman, who will expand his father's cocoa and chocolate business.

★ EVENTS Bedchamber Crisis: a political crisis which occurs after Melbourne, Prime Minister in the Whig government, offers to resign, and advises the young Queen Victoria to appoint Peel and the Tories. The Queen refuses to dismiss certain ladies of the Bedchamber with Whig sympathies, whereupon Peel refuses office and the Whig government continues.

First Opium War (to 1842): war between Britain and China over commercial rights in China, especially relating to the opium trade. Results in British victory.

Chartist riots in Newport, Wales.

1840

❀ BIRTHS Thomas Hardy: English novelist and poet.

★ EVENTS Treaty of Waitangi: the treaty that marks the formal assumption of sovereignty over New Zealand by the British government.

Young Ireland: an Irish protest movement which produces *The Nation* magazine, arguing for repeal of the Act of Union. It establishes an Irish Confederation in 1847, which returns several nationalists to parliament.

Kirkpatrick MacMillan builds the first bicycle, but, as he fails to patent it, it is widely copied.

1841

✿ BIRTHS   Edward VII: King of Great Britain, son of Queen Victoria.

✝ DEATHS   Sir David Wilkie: Scottish painter, renowned for genre painting in the Dutch style.

Sir Astley Cooper: English surgeon, famous for raising surgery from its primitive state to a science. He removed a tumour from the head of King George IV (1820).

★ EVENTS   Straits Convention: by this treaty, the Straits, the passage from the Bosphorus to the Dardanelles which links the Black Sea to the Mediterranean, is placed under international control. The treaty between the Great Powers (Britain, France, Austria, Prussia and Russia) closes the Straits to foreign warships during peacetime, a provision intended to reconcile Russian and British shipping interests since neither country will be able to menace the other's fleet on the Black Sea or the Mediterranean.

1842

✿ BIRTHS   Sir Arthur Sullivan: English composer, producer of the 'Gilbert and Sullivan' light operas in partnership with W S Gilbert.

✝ DEATHS   Sir Charles Bell: Scottish anatomist, surgeon and neurophysiological pioneer, who demonstrated that nerves consist of separate fibres sheathed together, and that fibres convey either sensory or motor stimuli but never both.

★ EVENTS   Chartist riots in Staffordshire and Lancashire.

British criminals sentenced to transportation for life may be sent to penal settlements. About 10 per cent of the 162,000 convicts transported to Australia were to spend some time in these settlements. Life in these settlements varies from unpleasant to savage, with hard labour and frequent and severe floggings.

Treaty of Nanjing: conclusion of the Opium War between China and Britain. The first of a series of unequal treaties that gives extensive privileges to foreign powers in China. Hong Kong is ceded to Britain in perpetuity.

Webster–Ashburton Treaty: an agreement between Britain and the USA which establishes the boundary between north-east USA and Canada.

1843

✳ EVENTS   Beginning of the Maori Wars (intermittently to 1872): a succession of conflicts in which the Maori people attempt, unsuccessfully, to resist the occupation of New Zealand by British settlers. The wars concern the settlers' demands for land and the growing opposition of a section of Maori opinion to land sales. Time and numbers, however, are on the side of the Europeans; Maori resistance is worn down, and they are forced to surrender or retreat to the wilder central North Island where pursuit is both difficult and unnecessary. An uneasy stand-off is reached by the early 1870s but peace is not formalized until 1881.

Disruption: Establishment of the Free Church of Scotland by Church of Scotland dissenters. The split occurs due to tensions between two groups within the established church — the Moderates and the Evangelicals. Although the Moderates had been dominant throughout the 18th century, by the 19th century the Evangelicals have gained influence and demand more freedom from the state and the right of congregations to elect their own ministers. Parliament denies these demands and the Evangelicals decide to split from the Church of Scotland. They do so at the General Assembly of the Church of Scotland, breaking away to form the Free Church of Scotland.

The SS *Great Britain* is launched in Bristol.

1844

✿ **BIRTHS**   Gerard Manley Hopkins: English poet.

✟ **DEATHS**   John Dalton: English chemist and natural philosopher. His development of the atomic theory of matter elevated chemistry to a quantitative science.

The Cooperative Society is founded in Rochdale.

1845

✿ **BIRTHS**   Thomas John Barnardo: Anglo-Irish founder of homes for destitute children, later known as the 'Barnardo Homes'.

✟ **DEATHS**   Charles Grey: British politician, Prime Minister in 1832 at the passage of the Reform Act.

★ **EVENTS**   Irish famine: the widespread starvation of Irish peasantry following the potato blight (1845–7) that destroys the crop. Due to resultant starvation and emigration (to Britain and the USA), the population of Ireland falls by almost 25 per cent between 1845 and 1851.

Sikh Wars (to 1846): first of two campaigns between the British and the Sikhs which lead to the British conquest and annexation of the Punjab, north-west India.

Sir John Franklin leads an expedition in search of the Northwest Passage (to 1847). Franklin and his crew all perish due to scurvy and starvation, but he is credited with the discovery.

1846

✿ **BIRTHS**   Michael Davitt: founder of the Irish Land League.

Charles Stewart Parnell: president of the Irish Land League.

✟ **DEATHS**   Thomas Clarkson: English philanthropist, crusader against African slavery. He was a leading member of the Anti-Slavery Society formed in 1823 for the abolition of slavery in the West Indies, which achieved its aim in 1833.

★ **EVENTS**   Growth of anti-British movement in Ireland.

Repeal of Corn Laws in Britain.

1847

✿ **BIRTHS**   Alexander Graham Bell: Scots-born US inventor, producer of the first intelligible telephonic transmission, and founder of the Bell Telephone company.

♱ **DEATHS**   Daniel O'Connell: Irish political leader, founder of the Repeal Association to agitate against Irish union with Britain.

Thomas Chalmers: Scottish theologian and reformer, leader of the 1843 Disruption, when 470 ministers withdrew from the Established Church of Scotland to found the Free Church of Scotland.

Sir John Franklin: English Arctic explorer credited with the discovery of the Northwest Passage. Dies of starvation and scurvy during the expedition.

✭ **EVENTS**   Factory Act: a maximum 10-hour working day for women and older children is enacted.

1848

✿ **BIRTHS**   Arthur Balfour: Scottish politician.

♱ **DEATHS**   George Stephenson: British inventor. He invented the locomotive and built the '*Rocket*', his most famous engine.

Emily Brontë: English novelist and poet, best known for her single novel *Wuthering Heights*, written under the pseudonym Ellis Bell. Dies of tuberculosis.

✭ **EVENTS**   Young Ireland rising in Tipperary is quelled.

Sikh Wars (to 1849): second of two campaigns between the British and the Sikhs which lead to the British conquest and annexation of the Punjab, north-west India.

Pre-Raphaelite Brotherhood: a group of artists forms in London in 1848 with the aim of revolutionizing early Victorian art; the name comes from their preference for the styles of the 15th century (ie pre-Raphael). Leading members are Sir John Everett Millais and Dante Gabriel Rossetti. They seek a new direct approach to nature, often inspired by Romantic poetry. Pre-Raphaelite Brotherhood pictures are recognizable by their bright colours, hard-edged forms, shallow picture-space, and meticulous attention to detail.

1849

✝ DEATHS   Anne Brontë: English novelist and poet. She wrote
her two novels, *Agnes Grey* and *The Tenant of Wildfell Hall*,
under the pseudonym Acton Bell. Dies of tuberculosis.

1850

❀ BIRTHS   Robert Louis Stevenson: Scottish writer.

✝ DEATHS   William Wordsworth: English poet.

Sir Robert Peel: English politician. Dies after a fall from his
horse.

★ EVENTS   The Stone Age village at Skara Brae in Orkney,
covered by a sandstorm in c.2300 BC, is uncovered by another
storm. Preserved relics are revealed which show the lifestyle
of the villagers who had abandoned the site during the earlier
storm.

(c.) Development of the system of crop rotation; the cultivation
of a number of different crops in a specified sequence on a
given area of land. The main object is to protect the fertility
of the soil. Rotations developed in Britain at this time usually
consist of three crops — a root crop (eg, potatoes), a grain
crop (eg, wheat) and a rest crop (eg, grass).

1851

✝ DEATHS   Mary Shelley: English writer, best known for her
novel *Frankenstein*.

Joseph Mallord William Turner: English landscape artist and
watercolourist.

★ EVENTS   Queen Victoria opens Hampton Court to the public;
its maze and gardens become huge tourist attractions.

Great exhibition housed in the Crystal Palace, London. Intended
to celebrate the 'Works of Industry of all Nations', in reality
it symbolizes Britain's mid-19th-century industrial
supremacy.

1852

❀ BIRTHS   Herbert Henry Asquith: English liberal politician and
Prime Minister of Britain.

✝ **DEATHS**   Duke of Wellington: Irish-born British general and politician. Defeated Napoleon I at the Battle of Waterloo.

Augustus Pugin: English architect, designer of a large part of the decorations and sculpture for the new Houses of Parliament (1836–7). A forerunner of the Gothic revival in England, he designed mainly Catholic churches.

★ **EVENTS**   David Livingstone discovers the Victoria Falls.

1854

❀ **BIRTHS**   Oscar Wilde: Irish writer.

✝ **DEATHS**   John Martin: English painter, who commonly used historical and Biblical themes.

★ **EVENTS**   Crimean War (to 1856): a war fought in the Crimean Peninsula by Britain and France against Russia. Its origins lie in Russian successes in the Black Sea area and the British and French desire to prevent further expansion into the Ottoman Empire by the Russians, since this would threaten the Mediterranean and overland routes to India. Results in Russian defeat.

Siege of Sevastopol (to 1855): the main engagement of the Crimean War. Britain, France, and Turkey attack Russia's main naval base in the Black Sea in order to reduce its alleged threat to the status quo in the Ottoman Empire and the Mediterranean. It takes 12 months and many casualties to capture Sevastopol.

(25 Oct) Battle of Balaclava: a battle fought between British and Russian forces during the early stages of the Crimean War. The Russian attack on the British base at Balaclava is unsuccessful, but the British sustain the heavier losses, due in part to the disastrous Charge of the Light Brigade.

1855

✝ **DEATHS**   Fergus O'Connor: Irish Chartist leader. He attempted to unify the Chartist movement via the National Charter Association, and presented himself as leader of the Chartist cause. Dies insane.

Charlotte Brontë: English novelist, most famed for her novel

Jane Eyre, written under the pseudonym Currer Bell. Dies during pregnancy.

1856

✿ BIRTHS   James Keir Hardie: Scottish Labour leader and founding member of the Labour Party.

Richard Haldane: Scottish politician, philosopher and lawyer.

George Bernard Shaw: Irish dramatist, essayist and pamphleteer.

✴ EVENTS   Second Opium War (to 1860): between Britain and China over commercial rights in China, especially relating to the opium trade. Britain is again victorious.

Treaty of Paris: the treaty bringing to an end the Crimean War. The Ottoman Empire is admitted to the so-called Concert of European Powers, but fails to keep its promise to respect the rights of its subjects.

Discovery of the process by which pig iron may be converted into steel.

1857

✿ BIRTHS   Joseph Conrad: Polish-born British novelist.

Sir Edward Elgar: English composer.

Robert Baden-Powell: British general and founder of the Boy Scout movement (1908) and the Girl Guides (1910).

✴ EVENTS   Foundation in New York of the Irish Republican Brotherhood (also known as the Fenians), a nationalist organization which espouses violence as a means of achieving its objective, and becomes best known for attacks in Manchester and London in 1867 to rescue imprisoned supporters. The fatalities which occur cause these to be called 'The Fenian Outrages'.

Indian Uprising (to 1858): a serious rebellion against British rule, triggered off partly by the belief among Indian troops in British service that new cartridges had been greased with animal fat, a concept abhorrent to Hindus and Muslims alike. At the same time, there is resentment among the old governing class over the reduction in their power, and Western innovations. The uprising at Meerut (10 May) spreads throughout northern India, with both urban and rural populations rising in revolt. Delhi quickly falls, and Kanpur and Lucknow garrisons are besieged. The British finally regain full control in mid-1858. The immediate result is the transfer of government from the British East India Company to the British Crown, but the long-term result is a legacy of bitterness on both sides.

1858

❀ BIRTHS   Emmeline Pankhurst: English suffragette, organizer of the Women's Social and Political Union and militant campaigner for women's suffrage.

✝ DEATHS   Robert Owen: Welsh social reformer, founder of a social welfare scheme and a model community with improved working and housing conditions at his New Lanark cotton mills.

Earl of Aberdeen: Scottish politician and Prime Minster of Britain.

John Snow: English anaesthetist and epidemiologist, identifier of the link between cholera and contaminated water supplies.

✫ EVENTS   Treaty of Tianjin: second unequal treaty imposed upon the Chinese by the Western powers following the Opium Wars. Facilitates expansion of foreign trade in China.

1859

❀ BIRTHS   Sir Arthur Conan Doyle: Scottish writer and creator of Sherlock Holmes.

Sydney Webb: English politician, social reformer, historian and economist.

John Jellicoe: English admiral.

✝ DEATHS   Isambard Kingdom Brunel: English engineer and inventor, designer of the Clifton and Hungerford Suspension Bridges and the ocean steamer the *Great Western*, until 1899 the largest vessel ever built.

1860

✿ **BIRTHS**   J M Barrie: Scottish novelist and playwright, author of *Peter Pan*.

1861

✿ **BIRTHS**   Sir William Burrell: Scottish ship owner and art collector.

Earl Douglas Haig: Scottish soldier and field marshal, founder of the Royal British Legion for the care of ex-servicemen.

✝ **DEATHS**   Albert, Prince consort of Queen Victoria. Dies of typhoid.

Richard Oastler: English social reformer, campaigner on behalf of the poor to improve their living and working conditions.

1862

✿ **BIRTHS**   Frederick Delius: British composer.

1863

✿ **BIRTHS**   David Lloyd George: Welsh Liberal politician and Prime Minister of Britain.

✝ **DEATHS**   William Makepeace Thackeray: English novelist, best known for *Vanity Fair*.

1865

✿ **BIRTHS**   George V: King of Great Britain, son of Edward VII.

Rudyard Kipling: British writer.

W B Yeats: Irish poet and dramatist.

✝ **DEATHS**   Henry Palmerston: English statesman.

Richard Cobden: English economist and politician, known as the Apostle of Free Trade. Founding member of the Anti-Corn Law League.

Sir William Hamilton: Irish mathematician.

1866

✿ **BIRTHS**   James Ramsay Macdonald: first British Labour Prime Minister.

Beatrix Potter: English writer and illustrator of children's books.

H G Wells: English writer.

1867

✿ BIRTHS   Stanley Baldwin: British politician and Prime Minister.

Arnold Bennett: English novelist.

✝ DEATHS   Michael Faraday: English chemist and physicist, his great life work was the series of *Experimental Researches on Electricity*, in which he described his many discoveries, including electromagnetic induction, the laws of electrolysis, and the rotation of the plane of polarized light by magnetism.

✦ EVENTS   Second Reform Act: gives the vote to all male settled tenants in the boroughs, thus creating a substantial working-class franchise for the first time.

British North America Act: an act passed by the British parliament which sanctions the Confederation of Nova Scotia, New Brunswick, Quebec and Ontario, giving rise to the Dominion of Canada. In 1982 it is renamed the Constitution Act.

East End Mission for Destitute Children established in London by John Barnardo — the first of the Barnardo homes.

1868

✿ BIRTHS   Charles Rennie Mackintosh: Scottish architect and designer.

Robert Falcon Scott: English Antarctic explorer.

1869

✿ BIRTHS   Neville Chamberlain: English statesman and Prime Minister of Great Britain.

1870

✝ DEATHS   Sir James Young Simpson: Scottish obstetrician, pioneer of chloroform as an anaesthetic, and the first to administer ether as an anaesthetic during labour.

Charles Dickens: English novelist.

★ EVENTS   First of the Irish Land Acts (to 1909): a succession of British Acts passed with the objective first of giving tenants greater security and compensation for improvements, and later of enabling tenants to buy the estates they farm. The Acts also aim to reduce nationalist grievances and agitation.

Founding of Fettes College, Edinburgh.

1871

❀ BIRTHS   Samuel John Peploe: Scottish painter, leading member of the Scottish Colourists.

✟ DEATHS   Charles Babbage: English mathematician, pioneer of the calculating machine, the forerunner of the computer.

1872

❀ BIRTHS   Ralph Vaughan Williams: English composer.

Arthur Griffith: Irish nationalist politician and founder of Sinn Féin.

1873

✟ DEATHS   John Stuart Mill: English philosopher and utilitarian reformer, supporter of female suffrage and liberalism.

David Livingstone: Scottish missionary and traveller.

Sir Edwin Landseer: English artist. Best known for his painting of a stag, *The Monarch of the Glen*.

1874

❀ BIRTHS   Winston Churchill: English statesman and Prime Minister of Britain. British premier during World War II.

Howard Carter: English archaeologist. Discoverer of the tomb of Tutankhamen.

John Duncan Fergusson: Scottish painter, one of the group of Scottish Colourists.

Gustav Holst: English composer.

1875

★ EVENTS   Alexander Graham Bell sends the first intelligible telephonic transmission.

Britain's Matthew Webb becomes the first man to swim the
English Channel.

1877

☨ DEATHS   William Henry Fox Talbot: English pioneer of
photography. He succeeded in making photographic prints
on silver chloride paper, which he termed 'photogenic
drawing', and later developed and patented the Calotype
process.

1878

☨ DEATHS   Sir George Gilbert Scott: English architect, the
leading practical architect of the British Gothic revival. He
was responsible for the building or restoration of many
ecclesiastical and civil buildings, including the Albert
Memorial, St Pancras Station and Hotel in London, and
Glasgow University.

1879

❀ BIRTHS   Viscountess Nancy Astor: first female Member of
Parliament.

William Henry Beveridge: British economist and social
reformer.

E M Forster: English novelist.

★ EVENTS   Formation of the Irish Land League by Michael
Davitt. The organization seeks fair rent and security of tenure
as well as the ability to sell property.

Zulu War: a war between British forces and the Zulu kingdom
characterized by initial reverses for the British but final defeat
for the Zulus. From the time of the arrival of Boer settlers in
northern Natal in 1836, there have been uneasy border
relations between white and black. The boundary is set at
different times but Boer farmers continue to penetrate
Zululand in search of land. A boundary commission is
appointed (1878), but the colonial authorities refuse to accept
its recommendations because they consider the terms to be
too favourable to the Zulus. When a party of Zulus crosses the
Natal border to kidnap two wives of a Zulu chief, war is
declared. After initial reverses, the British defeat the Zulus at

Ulundi. The removal of the Zulu military threat encourages the Boers to throw off British power in the Transvaal, leading to the first Boer War.

Tay Bridge Disaster: the rail bridge (opened 1 Jun 1878) across the River Tay at Dundee collapses during a severe gale. A train from Burntisland, Fife, with 75 people on board, is brought down with the bridge. There are no survivors.

1880

✿ BIRTHS   Marie Stopes: British suffragette and advocate of birth control. Founder of the first birth control clinic in London.

Sir Jacob Epstein: British sculptor.

✟ DEATHS   George Eliot (pseudonym of Mary Ann or Marian Evans): English novelist.

★ EVENTS   First Boer War (to 1881): first of two wars fought by the British and the Boers for the mastery of southern Africa. Ends with the defeat of the British at Majuba Hill, and the signing of the Pretoria and London Conventions of 1881 and 1884.

1881

✿ BIRTHS   Sir Alexander Fleming: Scottish bacteriologist, discoverer of the antibiotic powers of penicillin.

✟ DEATHS   Benjamin Disraeli: British politician and Prime Minister.

Thomas Carlyle: Scottish historian and man of letters. His best-known works include *Sartor Resartus*, on social philosophy, and *The French Revolution*.

★ EVENTS   Second of the Irish Land Acts (to 1909): a succession of British Acts passed with the objective first of giving tenants greater security and compensation for improvements, and later of enabling tenants to buy the estates they farm. The Acts also aim to reduce nationalist grievances and agitation.

(27 Feb) Battle of Majuba Hill: ends the first Boer War with Boer victory over the British.

Pretoria Convention: the agreement which concludes the first

Boer War, establishing limited independence for the Boers in the Transvaal.

1882

❀ BIRTHS   Eamon de Valera: Irish statesman and leader of the Irish Volunteers in the 1916 Easter Rising.

Virginia Woolf: English novelist.

James Joyce: Irish writer.

♱ DEATHS   Charles Darwin: English naturalist, his great work was *The Origin of Species by Means of Natural Selection* (1859), a controversial work that eventually succeeded in obtaining widespread recognition for the theory of natural selection.

Dante Gabriel Rossetti: English poet and painter, co-founder of the Pre-Raphaelite Brotherhood, which aimed to return to pre-Renaissance art forms involving vivid colour and detail.

★ EVENTS   (13 Sep) Battle of Tel el-Kebir: an engagement between British and Egyptian forces resulting in the British becoming the effective rulers of Egypt. It follows a period of increasing Egyptian ambition for extended power, which leads to a financial crisis.

Phoenix Park Murders: the murder in Dublin of the recently appointed Chief Secretary for Ireland, Lord Frederick Cavendish, and his under-secretary, Thomas Henry Burke, by a terrorist nationalist group called 'The Invincibles'. More murders follow during the summer. The British government responds with a fierce Coercion Act, which permits trials for treason and murder to take place before a judicial tribunal and without a jury, and gives police extensive additional search powers. Five of the Phoenix Park murderers are arrested and hanged.

1883

❀ BIRTHS   Clement Attlee: English Labour politician and Prime Minister.

John Maynard Keynes: English economist.

★ EVENTS   Government of India Acts (to 1935): measures passed by the British Parliament to regulate the government of India. They include the 1858 Act which transfers British

East India Company powers to the British Crown, and the 1919 and 1935 Acts which introduce limited constitutional change.

1884

✮ EVENTS   Third Reform Act: extends to rural and mining areas a franchise similar to that which, in 1867, gave the vote to all settled male tenants in the boroughs.

Foundation of the Imperial Federation League (to 1894): a British pressure group, with branches in Canada, working towards federation for the British Empire. Its members see this as an answer to the challenge of industrial powers such as Germany and the USA, to Britain's isolation within Europe, and to the rivalry with other imperial powers that emerges after 1880.

Foundation of both the London Society for the Prevention of Cruelty to Children (later the National Society for the Prevention of Cruelty to Children), and the Royal Scottish Society for the Prevention of Cruelty to Children.

1885

❀ BIRTHS   D H Lawrence: English novelist and poet.

✝ DEATHS   Anthony Shaftesbury: British factory reformer and philanthropist. Piloted the 1847 and 1859 Factory Acts through Parliament.

✮ EVENTS   Fourth Reform Act: aims to create parliamentary constituencies of broadly equal size.

1886

❀ BIRTHS   Siegfried Sassoon: English poet and novelist.

✮ EVENTS   British parliament rejects Irish Home Rule Bill.

1887

❀ BIRTHS   Rupert Brooke: English poet.

Edwin Muir: Scottish poet.

Dame Edith Sitwell: English poet.

Montgomery of Alamein: British field marshal, commander of

the British North-Africa campaign.

L S Lowry: English artist.

⭐ EVENTS   Bloody Sunday: the name conventionally given to clashes between police and demonstrators in Trafalgar Square, London, at a meeting called to protest against a ban on open-air meetings and to demand the release of an Irish MP who had been supporting a rent strike. Two demonstrators are killed. The meeting takes place against a background of economic depression, widespread unemployment and Irish nationalist unrest.

1888

❀ BIRTHS   John Logie Baird: Scottish electrical engineer and pioneer of television.

T S Eliot: US-born British poet, critic and dramatist.

⭐ EVENTS   Foundation of the Imperial British East Africa Company, a British company founded and chartered to rule a large area of East Africa. It is designed to ward off the German and French threats to the area and maintain British access to Lake Victoria, Uganda, and the upper Nile. However, it is seriously undercapitalized, and cannot find the resources to develop the region, create an infrastructure, or withstand African resistance. It winds up in 1894, and its territories become the protectorates (later Crown Colonies) of Kenya and Uganda.

Patenting of the pneumatic bicycle tyre by John Boyd Dunlop.

1889

❀ BIRTHS   Adolf Hitler: German dictator.

Charlie Chaplin: English film actor and director.

✝ DEATHS   John Bright: British politician and leading member of the Anti-Corn Law League. Closely associated with the Reform Act.

Robert Browning: English poet.

Gerard Manley Hopkins: English poet.

1890

❀ BIRTHS   Michael Collins: Irish politician and Sinn Féin leader.

1891

❀ BIRTHS   Agatha Christie: English mystery writer.

Sir Stanley Spencer: English painter. Religion will be his main
inspiration, with his works representing biblical events as
everyday life.

✝ DEATHS   Charles Stewart Parnell: president of the Irish Land
League, allied with the Liberals in support of Gladstone's
Home Rule Bill. Dies suddenly in Brighton.

1892

❀ BIRTHS   Hugh MacDiarmid (pseudonym of Christopher
Murray Grieve): Scottish poet.

Robert Alexander Watson-Watt: Scottish physicist and inventor
of 'Radio Detection and Ranging', or RADAR.

✝ DEATHS   Thomas Cook: British railway excursion and tourist
pioneer. His travel agency became a world-wide organization.

Alfred, Lord Tennyson: English poet.

Anthony Trollope: English novelist.

1893

❀ BIRTHS   Wilfred Owen: English poet of World War I.

✹ EVENTS   Independent Labour Party founded in Britain by
socialist Keir Hardie, with the objective of sending working
men to parliament. It is socialist in aim, but wishes to gain the
support of working people whether they are socialist or not.
Many of its leaders play a major part in founding the Labour
Representation Committee (1900), which becomes the
Labour Party in 1906. It is affiliated to the Labour Party but
puts up its own candidates, and is disaffiliated in 1932. It
continues to have a few members of parliament up to
1950.

1894

❀ BIRTHS Edward VIII: King of the United Kingdom, son of George V.

Harold Macmillan: English politician.

✝ DEATHS Robert Louis Stevenson: Scottish writer. Dies in Samoa.

Frances Mary Buss: English pioneer of higher education of women.

1895

❀ BIRTHS George VI: King of Great Britain, son of George V.

✫ EVENTS Foundation of the National Trust for Places of Historical Interest and Natural Beauty.

1896

✝ DEATHS Sir John Everett Millais: English painter, co-founder of the Pre-Raphaelite Brotherhood.

William Morris: English craftsman and poet, associated with the Pre-Raphaelite Brotherhood and a major figure in the Arts and Crafts Movement. He specialized in the revival of handicrafts and the art of house decoration and furnishing.

1897

❀ BIRTHS Aneurin Bevan: Welsh Labour politician. Architect of the National Health Service.

Anthony Eden: Anglo-Irish politician and Prime Minister of Britain.

Sir John Cockcroft: English nuclear physicist.

1898

❀ BIRTHS Dame Ninette de Valois: Irish ballerina and founder of the Royal Ballet.

Henry Moore: English sculptor.

✝ DEATHS Sir Edward Burne-Jones: English painter and designer, inspired by early Italian Renaissance. His paintings portray mainly Romantic and mythical subjects.

Lewis Carroll (pseudonym of Charles Lutwidge Dodgson):

English writer, was best known for his children's novel *Alice's Adventures in Wonderland* and its sequel, *Through the Looking Glass*.

William Ewart Gladstone: English politician and Prime Minister.

☆ EVENTS   Fashoda Incident: the settlement of Fashoda (now Kodok) on the upper White Nile is the scene of a major Anglo-French crisis. French forces reach the Nile after an 18-month journey from Brazzaville. The British, who are in the process of retaking the Sudan, issue an ultimatum; France is not prepared to go to war, and the forces are ordered to withdraw. The incident destroys French ambitions for a trans-continental African empire, and confirms British mastery of the Nile region.

1899

❀ BIRTHS   Noel Coward: English actor, playwright and composer.

Alfred Hitchcock: English film producer.

☆ EVENTS   Second Boer War: second of two wars fought by the British and the Boers for the mastery of southern Africa. The Boers effectively win the peace. They maintain control of 'native affairs', win back representative government in 1907, and federate South Africa on their terms in 1910. On the other hand, British interests in South Africa are protected and, despite internal strains, the Union of South Africa enters both World War I and World War II on the British side.

Bede: Anglo-Saxon scholar, historian and theologian (673–735), is canonized.

20th Century

British culture in the 20th century has reached a stage where its sheer size and diversity almost defies definition. The advances made in science and technology, the scope of change accelerated by the two World Wars and the development of new media of communication mean that 1900 and the present day have little in common to bind them.

All areas of culture are united in their struggle to break new ground. British art has not been so prone to the development of movements as it was previously, and as a result more stylistic tangents have been followed. This departure from the mainstream has led to constant controversy. Sir Jacob Epstein's series of 18 statues for the British Medical Association in 1907 caused public outrage, the portrait of Churchill by Graham Sutherland (official artist of World War II) so upset Lady Churchill that she had it destroyed, and moral and religious furore has continually surrounded Francis Bacon's emotive and disturbing images of the human figure.

British architecture of the 20th century has also had its share of controversy. Many of the social problems which arose in the years following World War II were blamed upon the high-rise towers and isolated housing estates which architects and planners considered the answer to the post-war housing shortage. The departure from traditionalism which has marked 20th-century architecture is reflected in movements such as International Modernism (which uses asymmetrical forms and cubic shapes) and Brutalism (which uses stark, exposed concrete structures) and has been widely criticised as unsympathetic and impractical.

British literature in the 20th century has been as vast and diverse as the influences it has absorbed. From the poets of World War I, such as Wilfred Owen and Siegfried Sassoon, who expressed the horror of war in graphic terms, British writers have been continually questioning the preconceived boundaries in which their predecessors worked. New standards have been set and broken, through the work of T S Eliot, Virginia Woolf, D H Lawrence and Samuel Beckett, to George Orwell, Hugh MacDiarmid and Salman Rushdie.

By far the most important cultural development and influence in the 20th century, however, is the emergence of television and cinema. Television fostered popular music and the two worked together as far as the musical phenomena of the 1960s were concerned. British cinema developed out of the silent film genius of Charlie Chaplin, through Alfred Hitchcock's excellence in suspense, to the work of David Lean and contemporary film makers such as Alan Parker, David Puttnam and Peter Greenaway.

1900

❀ BIRTHS   Prince Louis Francis of Battenburg, later Louis
      Mountbatten, great-grandson of Queen Victoria: British
      statesman and Admiral.

✝ DEATHS   John Ruskin: English writer and art critic.

   Oscar Wilde: Irish writer.

   Sir Arthur Sullivan: English composer, producer of the 'Gilbert
      and Sullivan' light operas in partnership with W S Gilbert.

✮ EVENTS   German Navy Act leads to massive increase in sea
      power and starts arms race with Britain.

   Foundation of the Labour Representation Committee, later the
      Labour Party: a socialist/social democratic political party,
      formed to represent trade unions and socialist societies as a
      distinct group in parliament.

1901

✝ DEATHS   Victoria: Queen of Great Britain and Empress of
      India, daughter of Edward, Duke of Kent.

1902

❀ BIRTHS   Stevie Smith: English poet and novelist.

✮ EVENTS   Anglo-Japanese Alliance (to 1921): the first modern
      alliance between a Western and Asian power. Takes account
      of each country's interests in China, as well as Japan's interests

in Korea, and provides for joint action in the event that either
of the signatories is involved in a war with more than one
power in East Asia. Each signatory would remain neutral if
the other fought only one power.

Peace of Vereeniging: the peace treaty which ends the Boer War,
signed at Pretoria. The Boers win three important
concessions: an amnesty for those who had risen in revolt
within the Cape Colony; a promise that the British will deny
the franchise to Africans until after the Boer republics are
returned to representative government; and additional
financial support for reconstruction. The peace ensures that
there will be no significant change in the political relationship
of whites and blacks in South Africa.

1903

❀ BIRTHS   Alec Douglas-Home: English politician and Prime
Minister of Britain.

Amy Johnson: English aviator and first woman to fly solo from
England to Australia.

George Orwell: English novelist and essayist.

Graham Sutherland: English artist.

Evelyn Waugh: English writer.

♰ DEATHS   Robert Cecil: English politician and Prime Minister
of Britain.

✺ EVENTS   Third of the Irish Land Acts (to 1909): a succession
of British Acts passed with the objective first of giving tenants
greater security and compensation for improvements, and
later of enabling tenants to buy the estates they farm. The
Acts also aim to reduce nationalist grievances and agitation.

1904

❀ BIRTHS   John Gielgud: English actor and director.

Graham Greene: English writer, author of many novels including
The Power and the Glory, *The Heart of the Matter*, *Brighton Rock*
and *The Third Man*. Dies 1991.

✺ EVENTS   Entente Cordiale agreed between Britain and France.

Foundation of Rolls-Royce: a British firm of car engine and

aero-engine manufacturers, founded by C S Rolls and Henry Royce.

1905

✝ DEATHS   Thomas John Barnardo: Anglo-Irish founder of homes for destitute children, later known as the 'Barnardo Homes'.

★ EVENTS   Formation of the Irish Nationalist Society, Sinn Féin, (literally, 'Ourselves Alone'), by Arthur Griffith, in support of Irish independence from Britain.

Establishment of the Camden Town Group (to 1913): a group of artists who flourish in London, sharing an enthusiasm for recent French painting.

1906

❀ BIRTHS   Samuel Beckett: Irish novelist, poet and playwright.

John Betjeman: English poet.

✝ DEATHS   Michael Davitt: founder of the Irish Land League.

★ EVENTS   26 MPs representing the Labour Representation Party are elected, and its name is changed to the Labour Party.

Establishment of the British Expeditionary Force (BEF): the army, sent to France (Aug 1914 and Sep 1939) to support the left wing of the French armies against German attack. In World War II its total strength was 394,000, of whom 224,000 were safely evacuated, mainly from Dunkirk, in May–June 1940.

Launching of HMS *Dreadnought*: a British battleship armed entirely with 'big guns', the production of which heralds the start of the pre-World War I naval race between Britain and Germany.

1907

❀ BIRTHS   Anthony Blunt: British double agent, art historian and Surveyor of the Queen's Pictures.

Daphne du Maurier: English novelist, best known for *Rebecca*.

Sir Basil Spence: Scottish architect.

Sir Frank Whittle: inventor of the jet engine.

Laurence Olivier: English actor, producer and director.

✝ DEATHS   William Thomson Kelvin: British physicist, who
   helped to develop the law of conservation of energy,
   established the second law of thermodynamics, and
   introduced the absolute (Kelvin) scale of temperature.

✮ EVENTS   Second Hague Peace Conference: Britain fails to
   secure arms limitations from Germany.

Anglo-Russian Entente (Dual Alliance): the Russian and British
   empires have been rivals in the Near, Middle and Far East
   for at least a century. However, they are gradually brought
   together by mutual distrust of an aggressive Germany and
   mutual interest in friendship with a worried France, with
   which Russia has had an alliance since 1894 and Britain an
   entente since 1904. Agreeing their respective spheres of
   influence, particularly in Persia, enables them to operate as a
   diplomatic bloc that goes to war united in 1914.

Triple Entente agreed between Britain, France and Russia.

Bloomsbury Group: a group of writers and artists who start
   meeting at about this time (to 1930) and take their name
   from Bloomsbury Square in London. They react against
   Victorian values and have a significant impact on the
   Modernist movement in England. They include Leonard and
   Virginia Woolf, Clive and Vanessa Bell, Maynard Keynes,
   and E M Forster.

1908

✝ DEATHS   Sir Henry Campbell-Bannerman: Scottish politician
   and Prime Minister of Britain.

✮ EVENTS   Foundation of the Boy Scout movement by Robert
   Baden-Powell.

Foundation of the Territorial Army: its volunteers receive
   continuous training on a part-time basis, and are intended to
   provide direct reinforcement to the British Army or to act in
   home defence.

1909

❀ BIRTHS   Francis Bacon: Irish artist. He will use repellent
images and repulsive human forms in his paintings. Dies
1992.

★ EVENTS   Fourth and final of the Irish Land Acts: a succession
of British Acts passed with the objective first of giving tenants
greater security and compensation for improvements, and
later of enabling tenants to buy the estates they farm. The
Acts also aim to reduce nationalist grievances and agitation.

1910

❀ BIRTHS   Norman MacCaig: Scottish poet.

Guy Burgess: British double agent.

✝ DEATHS   Edward VII: King of Great Britain, son of Queen
Victoria.

Florence Nightingale: British hospital reformer. She trained as
a nurse, and during the Crimean War (1854–6) had 10,000
patients under her care. She later formed an institution for
the training of nurses and spent several years on army sanitary
reform, the improvement of nursing and public health in
India.

W S Gilbert: English parodist and librettist of the 'Gilbert and
Sullivan' light operas in partnership with Sir Arthur Sullivan.

★ EVENTS   Robert Falcon Scott's expedition to the South Pole
(to 1912) is beaten by the Norwegians and all members of
the party perish.

Foundation of the Girl Guide movement by Robert Baden-
Powell.

1911

❀ BIRTHS   Sir John Charnley: British orthopaedic surgeon.

1912

❀ BIRTHS   Isaiah Berlin: British philosopher.

Jim Callaghan: English politician and Prime Minister of Britain.

Kim Philby: British double agent.

✞ DEATHS   Joseph Lister: English surgeon, pioneer of the
   antiseptic system, which revolutionized modern surgery.

Octavia Hill: English housing reformer and founder of the
   National Trust.

Robert Falcon Scott: English Antarctic explorer, beaten by the
   Norwegians in the race to the South Pole. Scott and all the
   members of his party perished on the expedition.

✸ EVENTS   British liner *Titanic* sinks after colliding with an
   iceberg; there are insufficient lifeboats and 1,513 passengers
   die.

1913

❀ BIRTHS   Benjamin Britten: English composer.

Roald Dahl: British writer.

✸ EVENTS   Threat of civil war in Ireland: Ulster Volunteers rise
   in opposition to proposed Home Rule Bill.

Establishment of the London Group: a society of British artists
   founded by Harold Gilman, Jacob Epstein and others. Holds
   regular exhibitions for half a century.

1914

❀ BIRTHS   Dylan Thomas: Welsh poet.

✸ EVENTS   World War I begins (to 1918): Britain declares war
   after Germany invades neutral Belgium. Britain is allied with
   France, Russia, Japan and Italy against Germany, Turkey and
   Bulgaria.

(6–12 Sep) First Battle of the Marne: offensive against the
   German army by the French army and the British
   Expeditionary Force. German plans for a quick, decisive
   victory on the Western Front are dashed by Allied victory. It
   is during this battle that the system of trench warfare which
   typifies World War I begins.

(19 Oct–22 Nov) Battle of Ypres (Passchendaele Campaign):
   Germany fails to break through the Western Front, despite
   the use of chlorine gas for the first time. Results in heavy loss
   of life.

Irish Home Rule Act provides for separate Parliament in Ireland.

Defence of the Realm Act ('DORA'): an Act introduced to give
the government greater controls over the activities of its
citizens. The most important control relates to restrictions on
press reporting and other forms of censorship. The
restrictions are increased as World War I progresses.

1915

✞ DEATHS   James Keir Hardie: founding member of the Labour
party and Scots Labour leader.

Rupert Brooke: English poet, inspired mainly by his experiences
of World War I. Dies of blood poisoning.

✯ EVENTS   Germany begins submarine blockade of Britain.

Gallipoli Campaign (to 1916): with stalemate on the Western
Front, the British War Council advocates operations against
the Turks to secure the Dardanelles (the straits into the Black
Sea) and aid Russia. The land campaign begins with
amphibious assaults on the Gallipoli Peninsula. Australian
and New Zealand forces are heavily involved, making the first
landing on 25 April and being repulsed by the Turks. Allied
casualties are 250,000 out of 480,000 engaged. The operation
is abandoned as a costly failure, with successful evacuations
of all remaining troops (Jan 1916).

(7 May) Sinking of the *Lusitania*: a Cunard passenger liner is
torpedoed by a German submarine off the Irish Coast while
in transit from New York to Liverpool, with 128 Americans
among the many lost. Although the German authorities argue
that the *Lusitania* was carrying war munitions for the Allies,
they do eventually make reparations. However, the sinking of
the liner causes worldwide anger and is instrumental in
bringing the USA into World War I.

(22–25 May) Second battle of Ypres and (9–25 May) Battle of
Artois. Allied offensives fail.

The first Women's Institute in Britain is founded at
Llanfairpwllgwyngyll, Wales.

1916

✿ BIRTHS   Edward Heath: English Conservative politician and
Prime Minister of Britain.

Harold Wilson: English Labour politician and Prime Minister of Britain.

Yehudi Menuhin: US-born British violinist, naturalized as a British Citizen in 1985.

Francis Crick: English molecular biologist, constructs a molecular model of the complex genetic material DNA with James Watson (1953); later, he will make far-reaching discoveries concerning the genetic code.

✸ EVENTS   Introduction of conscription.

(31 May–1 Jun) Battle of Jutland: World War I sea battle in which the British Grand Fleet from Scapa Flow intercepts the German High Seas Fleet off the west coast of Jutland, Denmark. Although the battle itself is inconclusive, German naval chiefs withdraw their fleet to port, and turn to unrestricted submarine warfare as a means of challenging British command of the sea.

(1 Jul–19 Nov) Battle of the Somme: British offensive against German troops in north-western France which develops into the bloodiest battle in world history, with more than a million casualties. It is launched by British Commander-in-Chief, Douglas Haig. When the attack is abandoned, the Allies have advanced 10 miles from previous positions. The battle is an excellent example of the futility of the war of attrition on the Western Front.

Easter Rising in Ireland: a rebellion of Irish nationalists in Dublin, organized by two revolutionary groups — the Irish Republican Brotherhood and Sinn Féin. Its focal point is the seizing of the General Post Office. After the rising is suppressed several leaders are executed, but the extent of the reprisals increase support for the nationalist cause in Ireland.

1917

✝ DEATHS   Elizabeth Garrett Anderson: British physician, pioneer for the admission of women into medicine and first woman mayor in England.

✸ EVENTS   (31 Jul–10 Nov) Battle of Passchendaele (third battle of Ypres): a British offensive which is continued despite no hope of achieving the original objective — a breakthrough to the Belgian ports. It is notable for appallingly muddy conditions, minimal gains, and British casualties of at least 300,000. In the final action, Canadians capture the village of Passchendaele, six miles north-east of Ypres.

Britain captures Bhagdad and Jerusalem from Turkey.

Balfour Declaration: Britain pledges support for a Jewish homeland in Palestine.

Foundation of the Co-operative Party: a political party which grows out of the ideas of voluntary mutual economic assistance developed in the 19th century by Robert Owen (1771–1858). One candidate, who joins with the parliamentary Labour Party, is elected to the House of Commons in 1918. Thereafter it becomes closely integrated with the Labour Party.

1918

✿ BIRTHS   Dennis Profumo: English politician, who will become infamous for his part in a scandal and will deceive the House of Commons about his relationship with Christine Keeler, a call girl also involved with a Soviet diplomat.

✝ DEATHS   Wilfred Owen: English poet of World War I. Killed in action one week before the armistice is signed.

✸ EVENTS   (15–18 Jul) Second Battle of the Marne: Germany's last offensive of the war, resulting in defeat.

End of World War I: Germany signs the armistice.

Civil war in Ireland (to 1923).

Reform Act: institutes universal male suffrage and gives the vote to women of 30 years and over.

Beginning of Allied Intervention in Russia (to 1922): the term refers to the intervention of foreign troops in Russian affairs following the Bolshevik October Revolution (1917). France, Britain, Japan and the USA are initially concerned to stiffen resistance to Germany by landing contingents in the north and the south of Russia and in eastern Siberia. Before these can become effective, however, Lenin concludes the separate Treaty of Brest-Litovsk (Mar 1918), and, instead, they are drawn into the Russian Civil War on the side of his opponents. This does nothing to help defeat Germany and sours

Western–Soviet relations for years to come. Most of the troops are withdrawn by 1920, but it is Oct 1922 before the Japanese leave Vladivostok.

Establishment of the Royal Air Force: the British air force, established from the combined forces of the Royal Flying Corps and the Royal Naval Air Service.

1919

✿ BIRTHS   Dame Margot Fonteyn: English ballerina. Dies 1991.

✭ EVENTS   The German fleet is scuppered in Scapa Flow, Orkney.

Peace conference begins in Paris, resulting in the Treaty of Versailles. The negotiations are dominated by Britain, the USA, France and Italy with none of the defeated nations being represented. The terms reduce the population and territory of Germany by approximately 10 per cent due to territorial redistribution and the fact that all German overseas colonies are taken over by the allies. The German army is restricted to 100,000 men, manufacture of armoured cars, tanks, submarines, aeroplanes and poison gas is restricted and all of Germany west of the Rhine is demilitarized. Most odious to the Germans is the War Guilt clause by which Germany has to accept full guilt for the war and pay reparations to the Allies for damage and losses sustained during the war.

Founding of the League of Nations. Its main aims are to preserve international peace and security by the prevention or speedy settlement of disputes and the promotion of disarmament. In 1946 its functions will be transferred to the United Nations (UN).

Formation of the Irish Republican Army (IRA): an anti-British paramilitary guerrilla force established by Irish nationalists to combat British forces in Ireland.

Lady Nancy Astor becomes the first female Member of Parliament.

Amritsar Massacre: in the course of agitation for Indian self-rule, riots break out in Amritsar in the Punjab. A gathering assembles three days later at Jallianwalla Bagh, a public park, on the festive occasion of Baisakhi. While they are being

addressed, the local British commander orders his troops to
fire on the unarmed crowd, killing 379 Indians and wounding
nearly 1,200. The long-term effect of the massacre is to drive
many Indians into supporting the Indian National Congress,
and M K Gandhi himself becomes convinced of the
impossibility of just rule under the British, and the necessity
for Indian independence.

1920

❀ BIRTHS   Roy Jenkins: Welsh politician and one of the 'Gang of
Four' who will establish the Social Democratic Party in 1981.

✷ EVENTS   Civil war in Ireland: Northern Ireland accepts the
Home Rule Act, resulting in two Irish Parliaments, one in
Belfast and one in Dublin.

Raising of the Black and Tans: additional members of the Royal
Irish Constabulary, recruited by the British government to
cope with Irish nationalist unrest. The shortage of regulation
uniforms leads to the recruits being issued with khaki tunics
and trousers and very dark green caps, hence their name.
Terrorist activities provoke severe and brutal reprisals by the
Black and Tans, which cause an outcry in Britain and the
USA.

Formation of the Communist Party of the UK.

1921

❀ BIRTHS   Prince Philip, son of Prince Andrew of Greece, great-
grandson of Queen Victoria, later Duke of Edinburgh,
husband of Queen Elizabeth II.

Robert Runcie: English Anglican Prelate and archbishop of
Canterbury.

✷ EVENTS   Establishment of the Irish Free State: a form of Home
Rule, established by the Anglo-Irish Treaty. Accordingly, 26
counties (excluding the six of Northern Ireland) become a
Dominion under the British crown and power is transferred
from Westminster (Mar 1922). The treaty is strongly opposed
by the Irish Republican Army.

Replacement of the Anglo-Japanese Alliance by a much looser

consultative Four-Power Pact (USA, Britain, France and Japan).

Reparations due from Germany to cover the cost of World War I set at £6,000m plus interest.

1922

✿ BIRTHS   Philip Larkin: English poet and novelist.

✝ DEATHS   Alexander Graham Bell: Scots-born US inventor, producer of the first intelligible telephonic transmission, and founder of the Bell Telephone company.

George Cadbury: English businessman. He expanded his father's cocoa and chocolate business, and established for the workers the model village of Bournville, a prototype for modern methods of housing and town planning.

Michael Collins: Irish politician and Sinn Féin leader. He became an MP in 1918, directed the guerrilla campaign during the Anglo-Irish War (1919–21), and was largely responsible for the negotiation of the Anglo-Irish Treaty with Great Britain in 1921. Dies in an ambush.

Arthur Griffith: Irish nationalist politician and founder of Sinn Féin.

✭ EVENTS   After the founding of the Irish Free State in 1921, the United Kingdom of Great Britain and Ireland is renamed the United Kingdom of Great Britain and Northern Ireland.

Republicans, led by Eamon De Valera, refuse to accept the authority of the crown following the Anglo-Irish Treaty of 1921 and civil war ensues. The Irish Republican Army is suppressed by the Irish government.

Labour Party overtakes Liberals as main party in opposition.

1923

✭ EVENTS   Foundation of Fine Gael: Irish political party created out of the pro-Anglo-Irish Treaty wing of Sinn Féin.

1924

✝ DEATHS   Joseph Conrad: Polish-born British novelist, whose best-known works include the novel *Lord Jim* and the short story *Heart of Darkness*.

✸ EVENTS   First British Labour government under Ramsay
Macdonald.

1925

❀ BIRTHS   Margaret Thatcher: Conservative MP and the first
British female party leader and Prime Minister.

✸ EVENTS   Locarno Pact: series of agreements by which Britain,
Germany, France, Italy and Belgium agree to arbitration in
an attempt to guarantee peace in Western Europe.

Foundation of Plaid Cymru: the Welsh National Party, founded
with the aim of achieving independence for Wales.

John Logie Baird gives his first demonstration of television in
London.

1926

❀ BIRTHS   Reverend Ian Paisley: Northern Irish militant
Protestant clergyman and politician.

Elizabeth II, daughter of George VI, and later Queen of the
United Kingdom of Great Britain and Northern Ireland
(Elizabeth II of England).

✸ EVENTS   (4–12 May) General strike in Britain: a national strike
organized by the Trades Union Congress (TUC) in support
of an existing miners' strike to resist wage cuts. The
government organizes special constables and volunteers to
counter the most serious effects of the strike, and issues an
anti-strike propaganda journal, *The British Gazette*. The TUC
call off the strike, though the miners' strike continues
fruitlessly for three more months.

Eamon De Valera founds Fianna Fáil: an Irish political party
founded in opposition to the 1921 Anglo-Irish Treaty.

1927

✸ EVENTS   Launch of BBC Radio.

1928

♱ DEATHS   Herbert Henry Asquith: English liberal politician and
Prime Minister of Britain.

Richard Haldane: Scottish politician, philosopher and lawyer.

As Secretary of State for War he remodelled the army and later founded the territorial army and co-founded the London School of Economics.

Thomas Hardy: English novelist and poet, author of *Tess of the D'Urbervilles*, *Far From the Madding Crowd* and *The Mayor of Casterbridge*.

Earl Douglas Haig: Scottish soldier and field marshal, founder of the Royal British Legion for the care of ex-servicemen.

Charles Rennie Mackintosh: Scottish architect and designer. Architect of the Glasgow School of Art and Hill House in Helensburgh.

Emmeline Pankhurst: English suffragette, organizer of the Women's Social and Political Union and militant campaigner for women's suffrage. She was frequently imprisoned and also undertook hunger strikes. After the outbreak of World War I, she turned her attention to the industrial mobilization of women.

✰ EVENTS   Fall in wheat prices heralds huge economic slump.

Reform Act: gives the vote to all women aged 21 and over.

Foundation of the Scottish National Party: formed as the National Party of Scotland, it merges with the Scottish Party in 1934. Its principal policy aim is independence for Scotland from the UK.

Alexander Fleming discovers the antibiotic powers of penicillin.

1929

✾ BIRTHS   Roger Bannister: English athlete and first man to run a mile in under four minutes.

✰ EVENTS   Great Depression (to 1935): a worldwide slump in output and prices, and greatly increased levels of unemployment (2.8 million in Britain in 1932), precipitated by the collapse of the US stock market (the Wall Street crash) in Oct 1929. This ends US loans to Europe and greatly reduces business confidence worldwide.

Colonial Development and Welfare Acts: a series of acts (to 1950) designed to offer funds for the development of British colonies. They represent a departure from the notion that colonies should be self-supporting and a recognition that development might serve to combine colonial idealism with British economic self-interest.

1930

✿ BIRTHS   Shirley Williams: English politician and one of the 'Gang of Four' who will establish the Social Democratic Party in 1981.

✝ DEATHS   Arthur Balfour: Scottish politician, responsible for the Balfour Declaration which promised Zionists a home in Palestine.

Sir Arthur Conan Doyle: Scottish writer and creator of Sherlock Holmes.

D H Lawrence: English novelist and poet.

✹ EVENTS   End of occupation of Germany by Allied troops.

Adoption of the political strategy of civil disobedience by M K Gandhi and his followers in India, in opposition to Britain's imperial rule. Launched by a march to the coast in order to break the law symbolically by making salt (on which tax is payable), it is a non-violent, mass, illegal protest, intended to discredit the authority of the state. The movement is banned, and many are arrested, including Gandhi.

St Kilda, a group of small volcanic islands in the Atlantic Ocean, 100 miles west of the Scottish mainland, is abandoned, after having been inhabited for 2,000 years.

1931

✝ DEATHS   Arnold Bennett: English novelist.

✹ EVENTS   Statute of Westminster: legislation which clarifies that Dominions in the British Empire are autonomous communities and effectively independent, though owing common allegiance to the crown. Establishes a free association of members in the 'Commonwealth of Nations'.

1932

✿ BIRTHS   Albert Reynolds: Irish politician and Prime Minister.

✫ EVENTS   Fianna Fáil (formed in opposition to the 1921 Anglo-Irish Treaty) comes to power with Eamon De Valera as Prime Minister. It has been the governing party for most of the period since, emphasizing separation from Britain during the 1930s, and consistently supporting the unification of Ireland.

1933

❀ BIRTHS   Michael Heseltine: English politician.

✫ EVENTS   Adolf Hitler appointed Chancellor of Germany; results in German withdrawal from the League of Nations.

1934

❀ BIRTHS   Chris Bonington: English mountaineer, member of the British team that takes part in the first successful conquest of the north face of the Eiger (1962) and leader of the expedition which makes the first ascent of the south-west face of Everest (1975).

✝ DEATHS   Sir Edward Elgar: English composer of the *Pomp and Circumstance* marches (the first of which is *Land of Hope and Glory*), the *Enigma Variations* and *The Dream of Gerontius*.

Frederick Delius: English composer of German Scandinavian origin. His works include *A Village Romeo and Juliet* and *A Song of Summer*.

Gustav Holst: English composer of Swedish origin, most famous for his seven movement suite, *The Planets*.

✫ EVENTS   Opening of the opera house at Glyndebourne, site of one of Britain's most famous music festivals.

Founding of Gordonstoun School, Moray.

1935

✝ DEATHS   Samuel John Peploe: Scottish painter, one of the Scottish Colourists.

John Jellicoe: English admiral, Commander-in-Chief at the outbreak of the First World War and during the Battle of Jutland.

✫ EVENTS   Hitler denounces Treaty of Versailles and starts process of rearmament.

Conference of Stresa: following Hitler's declaration of German rearmament, the Italian, French and British governments condemn the move at a meeting in Stresa. They guarantee Austria's independence and agree on future co-operation (Stresa Front). The Front is quickly undermined by the Anglo-German Naval Treaty (18 Jun), by which Germany may have no more than 35 per cent of Britain's tonnage, and Italy's invasion of Abyssinia and intervention in the Spanish Civil War.

1936

✝ **DEATHS**   George V: King of the United Kingdom, son of Edward VII.

Rudyard Kipling: English writer, best known for *Barrack Room Ballads*, the two *Jungle Books* and the *Just So Stories*.

★ **EVENTS**   Edward VIII, King of the United Kingdom, abdicates to marry American divorcee Wallis Simpson.

Jarrow March: a march to London by unemployed workers from the Durham shipbuilding and mining town, to put the case for the unemployed. Jarrow is among the towns worst affected by the Depression, and the march takes place at a time when the economy is recovering in much of the rest of the country. It alerts the more prosperous South and Midlands to the intractable problems of depressed areas.

The Irish Republican Army is banned by Irish Prime Minster Eamon De Valera, and remains largely inactive until the 1960s.

Launch of BBC Television.

1937

❀ **BIRTHS**   David Hockney: English artist, associated with the Pop Art movement.

✝ **DEATHS**   Ramsay Macdonald: first British Labour Prime Minister.

J M Barrie: Scottish novelist and playwright, author of *Peter Pan*.

★ **EVENTS**   Peel Commission: the report of this commission is famous (or notorious) for being the first formal recommendation of the partition of Palestine into separate states, Arab and Jewish, with the retention by the British of a corridor to the Mediterranean. Serious rioting by the Arabs, directed against the Jews, leads Stanley Baldwin, the British Prime Minister, to appoint a royal commission to enquire into the working of the British mandate under the leadership of Earl Peel. Despite the commission's evident recognition that there is a serious problem in Palestine its recommendations find favour with only some Arabs and Zionists, and are rejected by the British House of Lords

1938

✿ BIRTHS   John Smith: Scottish politician and leader of the Labour Party. Dies 1994.

David Steel: Scottish politician, and leader of the Liberal Party.

Arthur Scargill: English Trade Union leader.

✪ EVENTS   Munich Agreement: Munich pact signed by Hitler (Germany), Mussolini (Italy), Chamberlain (Britain) and Daladier (France); gives Czech Sudetenland to Germany, allegedly in the interest of European peace.

1939

✿ BIRTHS   Seamus Heaney: Irish poet.

Terry Waite: later English religious adviser to the Archbishop of Canterbury.

♱ DEATHS   Howard Carter: English archaeologist. His discoveries included the tombs of Hatshepsut, Tuthmosis IV and, most notably, that of Tutankhamen.

W B Yeats: Irish poet and dramatist.

✪ EVENTS   The IRA begin a bombing campaign on mainland Britain.

Introduction of conscription for 20–21-year-old men.

Hitler invades Poland, despite warnings from Britain and France that they will protect it. War is declared.

Introduction of compulsory conscription for 18–41-year-old men.

Discovery of the Sutton Hoo ship burial: the grave of an Anglo-Saxon king, probably Raedwald of East Anglia (d.624/5), discovered beneath a barrow on the River Deben near

Woodbridge, East England. Excavations reveal a 40-oar open
rowing boat with a wooden burial chamber containing silver
plate, gold jewellery, coins, weapons, and domestic
equipment (now in the British Museum).

1940

✝ DEATHS   Neville Chamberlain: English statesman and Prime
Minster of Great Britain.

✮ EVENTS   (27 May–3 Jun) Retreat from Dunkirk: as German
forces push forward through France and Belgium, the British
Expeditionary Force and the First French Army are cut off
near Dunkirk. British warships and boats rescue nearly
340,000 men from the beaches under intense German attack.

(2 Jun 1940–Apr 1941) Battle of Britain: the name given to the
air war campaign in which the German Luftwaffe attempts to
destroy the Royal Air Force as a prelude to the invasion of
Great Britain. The aerial offensive begins in August, with the
German bomber aircraft and fighter escorts concentrating on
wiping out the RAF both by combat in the air and by bombing
their vital airfields in the south of the country. British
resistance proves stubborn, and the Luftwaffe switch their
offensive from attacks on airfields to attacks on British cities
(the 'Blitz'), losing their opportunity to gain true air
superiority. Between 1 July and 31 October the Luftwaffe lose
2,848 aircraft to the RAF's 1,446.

The Blitz: the colloquial name for the series of air raids on
British cities by the German Air Force (Sep 1940–May 1941).
The purpose of the raids is to weaken British resistance to
projected invasion. The cities of London and Coventry are
particularly badly affected.

Neville Chamberlain resigns as Prime Minister and is replaced
by Winston Churchill.

Battle of the Atlantic begins (to 1943): the German strategy is
to cut off Britain's supplies of food and munitions by
submarine action. Only at the end of 1943 are the attacks
countered, and the threat brought under control.

Rationing is introduced for essential items such as food, petrol
and clothing.

1941

✿ BIRTHS   Paddy Ashdown: English politician and leader of the
Liberal Democrat Party.

✟ DEATHS   James Joyce: Irish writer. His seminal novel *Ulysses*
was not published in the United Kingdom until 1936.

Virginia Woolf: English novelist. With James Joyce, she is
regarded as one of the great modern innovators of the novel
in English.

Robert Baden-Powell: British general and founder of the Boy
Scout movement (1908) and the Girl Guides (1910).

Amy Johnson: English aviator and first woman to fly solo from
England to Australia. Drowns after baling out over the
Thames Estuary.

✭ EVENTS   The war is costing Britain £11m a day, but
Churchill's government still receives a vote of confidence.

Britain receives first shipments of food from the USA.

War is declared on Finland, Romania and Hungary.

Anglo-Soviet invasion of Iran: suspicions that Iran is sympathetic
to the Germans in World War II result in the Anglo-Soviet
invasion, although it is possible that a desire to protect oil
supplies among other things is also a motive for the invasion
on the British side. The country will be subjected to Anglo-
Soviet military occupation until 1946.

1942

✿ BIRTHS   Neil Kinnock: Welsh politician and leader of the
Labour party.

Stephen Hawking: English theoretical physicist, whose research
on relativity will spark his major contributions to the theory
of the 'Big Bang' (on how the universe was created), and to
current knowledge of black holes. His book *A Brief History of
Time* (1988) is a bestselling popular account of modern
cosmology.

✭ EVENTS   (23 Oct–4 Nov) Battle of El Alamein: a battle, named
after a village on Egypt's Mediterranean coast, which ends in
the victory of the British Eighth Army commanded by
Montgomery over Rommel's Afrika Corps. It proves to be a

turning point in the war in Africa, and begins the allied offensive in Egypt.

William Beveridge's Report on *Social Insurance and Allied Services* recommends social insurance for all, and forms the basis of the welfare state.

Quit India Movement: a campaign launched by the Indian National Congress calling for immediate independence from Britain, and threatening mass non-violent struggle if its demands are not met. M K Gandhi and other Congress leaders are arrested, and the movement is suppressed, though not without difficulty and more than 1,000 deaths. It contributes significantly to the eventual decision by Britain to withdraw from India soon after the end of World War II.

1943

🐝 BIRTHS   John Major: English Conservative politician and Prime Minister of Britain.

♱ DEATHS   Beatrix Potter: English writer and illustrator.

★ EVENTS   British daily expenditure on war is estimated at £14m.

Berlin, Stuttgart, Rome, Milan and Turin are bombed by the RAF.

Part-time work is made compulsory for all British women aged 18–45.

Italy surrenders to the Allies.

1944

🐝 BIRTHS   Ranulph Fiennes: English polar explorer.

★ EVENTS   School-leaving age raised to 15.

(6 Jun) D-Day: the day when the Allies launch the greatest amphibious operation in history (code-named 'Overlord'), and invade German-occupied Europe. By the end of D-Day, 130,000 troops have been landed on five beach-heads along a 50 mile stretch of the coast of Normandy, at a cost of 10,000 casualties.

Normandy Campaign: World War II campaign which begins on D-Day. Allied forces under the command of General

Eisenhower begin the liberation of Western Europe from
Germany by landing on the Normandy coast between the
Orne River and St Marcouf. Artificial harbours are
constructed along a strip of beach so that armoured vehicles
and heavy guns can be unloaded. Heavy fighting ensues for
three weeks, before Allied troops capture Cherbourg (27
Jun). Tanks break through the German defences, and Paris is
liberated (25 Aug), followed by the liberation of Brussels (2
Sep), and the crossing of the German frontier (12 Sep).

Government begins evacuation of children from London due to
the danger posed by German bombing.

(17–25 Sep) Battle of Arnhem: a major conflict in occupied
Dutch territory towards the end of World War II, in which
the German forces thwart Allied attempts to break through.
The operation involves the largest airlift operation of the war,
parachuting 10,000 troops into the Dutch rivers area, to take
key bridges over the Rhine, Maas and Waal. Allied forces
advance to Nijmegen, but at Arnhem meet the 9th and 10th
German Panzer divisions, which successfully resist attack and
eventually force an Allied withdrawal to behind the Rhine
River.

(16 Dec–late Jan) Battle of the Bulge: the last desperate German
armoured counter-offensive through the Ardennes in World
War II to prevent the Allied invasion of Germany. It achieves
early success but grinds to a halt, and the Germans are forced
to retreat by the Allies.

Sir William Burrell gives his collection of over 8,000 works of
art to the city of Glasgow, with provision for a gallery.

1945

✝ DEATHS   Adolf Hitler, German dictator: commits suicide with
his new bride, Eva Braun, in an air raid shelter under the
chancellory building in Berlin following Allied invasion of
Germany.

David Lloyd George: Welsh Liberal politician and Prime
Minister of Britain.

✰ EVENTS   100,000 civilians die after Allied bombing of
Dresden.

Belsen concentration camp in North Germany liberated by the British.

The Second World War officially ends, following Hitler's suicide.

Atomic bombs are dropped on Hiroshima and Nagasaki by the US following Japanese refusal to surrender. Results in Japanese full surrender and final conclusion of the war.

The first majority Labour government under Clement Attlee (to 1951): establishes the welfare state and carries out a significant nationalization programme.

Conscription is converted to National Service.

Beginning of the Nuremberg Trials: proceedings held by the Allies at Nuremberg after World War II to try Nazi war criminals. An International Military Tribunal is set up, and sits from Nov 1945 until Oct 1946. The Nazis tried in person number 21, including Hermann Goering and Joachim Von Ribbentrop (who are sentenced to death), and Rudolf Hess (who is given life imprisonment).

Foundation of the United Nations (UN): an organization formed to maintain world peace and foster international co-operation.

The Scottish National Party wins its first seat at a by-election.

1946

✝ DEATHS   H G Wells: English writer, author of *The Time Machine* and *War of the Worlds*.

John Maynard Keynes: English economist. The unemployment crises inspired his two major works, *A Treatise on Money* and the revolutionary *General Theory of Employment, Interest and Money*.

John Logie Baird: Scottish electrical engineer and pioneer of television.

★ EVENTS   Paris Peace Conference (to 1947): meetings of the five members of the Council of Foreign Ministers, representing the main World War II Allies (USA, Russia, UK, France and China), and delegates from 16 other nations involved against the Axis Powers. It draws up peace treaties with Bulgaria, Finland, Hungary, Romania and Italy. Despite repeated divisions, agreement is finally reached and the treaties signed in the spring of 1947.

1947

❀ BIRTHS Salman Rushdie: British writer born in India, author of *The Satanic Verses* and *Midnight's Children*.

✝ DEATHS Stanley Baldwin: British politician and Prime Minister.

Sydney Webb: English politician, social reformer, historian and economist. Husband of Beatrix Potter.

★ EVENTS Transport Act creates British Rail.

Founding of the Edinburgh International Festival.

Founding of the Aldeburgh Festival with the development of the English Opera Group under the influence of Benjamin Britten.

1948

❀ BIRTHS Charles: heir apparent to the British throne, son of Queen Elizabeth II, later invested as Prince of Wales.

Gerry Adams: Northern Irish politician and president of Sinn Féin.

★ EVENTS Establishment of National Health Service by Minister of Health, Aneurin Bevan. Its stated aim is to provide free health care and it is funded by national government and local taxation.

Establishment of a Jewish state.

Declaration of the Irish Republic by the Republic of Ireland Act: comes into effect in 1949. It changes the relationship between Ireland and Britain. The republic retains special citizenship arrangements and trade preference with Britain, but leaves the Commonwealth of Nations. Northern Ireland will remain part of the UK until its citizens declare otherwise.

1949

★ EVENTS North Atlantic Treaty Organization (NATO) formed by Western Allies. Includes Belgium, Canada, Denmark, France, Iceland, Italy, Luxembourg, the Netherlands, Norway, Portugal, the UK and the USA, and later Greece, Turkey, West Germany and Spain. NATO is a permanent military alliance established to defend Western Europe against Soviet aggression. The treaty commits the members to treat an armed attack on one of them as an attack on all of them, and for all to assist the country attacked by such actions as are deemed necessary.

1950

✿ BIRTHS   Princess Anne, daughter of Queen Elizabeth II, later the Princess Royal.

✟ DEATHS   George Bernard Shaw: Irish dramatist, essayist and pamphleteer. A famous vegetarian, he lived to the age of 94, and wrote many notable plays.

George Orwell: English novelist and essayist, best known for *1984* and *Animal Farm*.

✯ EVENTS   Tripartite Declaration: represents an attempt by Britain, France and the USA to limit arms supplies to Israel and the Arab states in the wake of the emergence of the state of Israel, in the hope that this will ensure some stability for the area. Arms supplies are to be conditional on non-aggression, and the signatories to the Declaration undertake to take action both within and outside the framework of the UN in cases of frontier violation.

1951

✯ EVENTS   Opening of the Festival of Britain by George VI.

Beginning of introduction of National Health Service charges, subsequently extended to include many prescriptions, most dental treatments and eye tests.

1952

✟ DEATHS   George VI: King of the United Kingdom, son of George V. Dies suddenly of coronary thrombosis.

✯ EVENTS   Foundation of the European Community (EC): a community of 12 states in Western Europe created for the purpose of achieving economic and political integration.

1953

✟ DEATHS   Dylan Thomas: Welsh poet, author of *Under Milk Wood*. Dies as a result of alcohol abuse.

1955

✟ DEATHS   Sir Alexander Fleming: Scottish bacteriologist, the first to use anti-typhoid vaccines on humans. He made early use of the new treatment salvarsan, a compound of arsenic for syphilis, and discovered the antiseptic powers of lysozyme. Most famous for his discovery of the antibiotic powers of penicillin.

✭ EVENTS   Cardiff becomes the official capital of Wales.

1956

✭ EVENTS   Suez Crisis: a political crisis focused on the Suez Canal. Intensive rearmament by Egypt, the Egyptian nationalization of the Suez Canal, and the establishment of a unified command with Jordan and Syria aiming to surround and eliminate Israel, leads in October to a pre-emptive strike by Israel in Sinai. Following this attack, the UK and France ask both sides to withdraw from the Canal Zone and agree to temporary occupation. When this is rejected by Egypt, the British and French invade, but have to withdraw following diplomatic action by the USA and USSR. Israel is also forced to relinquish the Sinai Peninsula. There have been many allegations of collusion between Israel, France and the UK.

The Sadler's Wells Ballet receives a royal charter and becomes the Royal Ballet.

1957

❀ BIRTHS   John McCarthy: English journalist, later to be held hostage in Beirut for 1,943 days.

1958

✟ DEATHS   Sir William Burrell: Scottish ship owner and art collector.

Ralph Vaughan Williams: English composer.

Marie Stopes: British suffragette and advocate of birth control, founder of the first birth control clinic in London.

★ EVENTS   Formation of CND (Campaign for Nuclear Disarmament) to oppose Britain's development of a nuclear weapons programme. It organizes annual marches and briefly persuades the Labour Party to declare a policy of unilateral disarmament in 1960, only to see it effectively reverse that decision a year later. It remains an influential pressure group in the 1960s, though its popularity begins to decline before the signing of nuclear non-proliferation pacts in the 1980s.

European Economic Community (EEC) established by the Treaty of Rome, original members are France, Belgium, Luxemburg, The Netherlands, Italy and West Germany. It is essentially a customs union, with a common external tariff and a common market with the removal of barriers to trade among the members.

Notting Hill Riots: a series of violent demonstrations in north-west London. Directed at non-white immigrants living there, they bring the issue of immigration into the British political arena for the first time.

Britain's first motorway, the Preston Bypass, is opened.

1959

✟ DEATHS   Edwin Muir: Scottish poet.

Sir Stanley Spencer: English painter. His main inspiration was religion, and his major works represent biblical events as everyday life.

Sir Jacob Epstein: British sculptor.

1960

❀ BIRTHS   Prince Andrew, son of Queen Elizabeth II, later Duke of York.

✟ DEATHS   Aneurin Bevan: Welsh Labour politician. Architect of the National Health Service.

★ EVENTS   Foundation of the National Front (NF): a strongly nationalist political party which centres its political programme on opposition to immigration, and calls for the repatriation of ethnic minorities even if they were born in the

UK. The party is created by the merger of the White Defence League and the National Labour Party, and in its early years is a small neo-Nazi grouping. Its political appeal declines with the election of a Conservative government in 1979.

Penguin Books are unsuccessfully prosecuted in a highly publicized obscenity trial following their publication of D H Lawrence's *Lady Chatterley's Lover*, criticized for its language and sexual explicitness.

1961

❀ BIRTHS   Diana Spencer, later Princess of Wales, wife of Charles, Prince of Wales.

♱ DEATHS   John Duncan Fergusson: Scottish painter, one of the group of Scottish Colourists. He is best known for his series of World War I paintings of naval dockyards, and his portraits of the female nude.

★ EVENTS   Foundation of Amnesty International: a British-based pressure group that campaigns for the release of any person detained for their political or religious beliefs or who has been unjustly imprisoned for any other reason.

1962

★ EVENTS   Abolition of National Service.

1963

♱ DEATHS   William Henry Beveridge: British economist, social reformer and author of *Report on Social Insurance and Allied Services* (the Beveridge Report), which helps to create the welfare state.

Guy Burgess: British double agent. Dies in Moscow after his defection.

★ EVENTS   Nuclear test ban treaty signed by Britain, USA and Russia as an indirect means of slowing down the proliferation of countries with nuclear weapons.

The Great Train Robbery: the night mail train transferring high value packages from Glasgow to London is stopped by a gang of robbers (which include Ronald Biggs) at Sears Crossing in Buckinghamshire. They escape with 120 mailbags, containing over £2.5m, but are traced and arrested after their fingerprints are found in a farm hideout.

1964

❀ **BIRTHS**   Prince Edward, son of Queen Elizabeth II.

✝ **DEATHS**   Viscountess Nancy Astor: first female Member of Parliament.

Dame Edith Sitwell: English poet.

★ **EVENTS**   Completion of the Forth Road Bridge, spanning the Forth River near Edinburgh.

1965

✝ **DEATHS**   Winston Churchill: English statesman and Prime Minister of Britain. British premier during the World War II.

T S Eliot: US-born British poet, critic and dramatist. Became a naturalized British citizen in 1927. Best known for his poems *The Love Song of J. Alfred Prufrock*, *The Wasteland* and *Four Quartets*.

★ **EVENTS**   Rhodesia Crisis: a series of events that begins with the announcement by Prime Minister Ian Smith of a Unilateral Declaration of Independence (11 Nov 1965). This follows the Rhodesian Government's failure to agree with successive British Administrations on a constitutional independence settlement that will ensure the continuance of white supremacy.

1966

✝ **DEATHS**   Evelyn Waugh: English writer, author of *Brideshead Revisited*.

★ **EVENTS**   144 people killed, including 116 children, when a landslip of mining waste engulfs several houses and a school in Aberfan, a village in a coal-mining region of Mid Glamorgan, South Wales.

1967

✝ **DEATHS**   Clement Attlee: English Labour politician and Prime Minister.

Siegfried Sassoon: English poet and novelist, who drew

inspiration from his experiences in World War I.

Sir John Cockcroft: English nuclear physicist. He induced the first artificial disintegration of a nucleus by bombarding a lithium nucleus with protons (1932), pioneering the use of particle accelerators.

1968

☆ EVENTS   Nuclear Non-Proliferation Treaty (NPT): a treaty signed by the USA, the USSR, the UK and an open-ended list of over 100 other countries. It seeks to limit the spread of nuclear weapons, with those possessing them agreeing not to transfer the capability to produce them, and those not possessing them agreeing not to acquire the capability.

1969

☆ EVENTS   British troops sent to Northern Ireland to quell trouble arising from a People's Democracy march from Belfast to Londonderry.

A major split in the ranks of the Irish Republican Army leads to the formation of the Provisional IRA alongside the Official IRA, and a serious schism between the two sides in the early 1970s. The Official IRA is virtually inactive after 1972, and generally supports political action to achieve Irish unity. The Provisionals become the dominant republican force, responsible for shootings and bombings in Northern Ireland, Britain, and Western Europe. Targets are mainly security and military personnel and establishments, although there are also many sectarian killings and attempts to disrupt civilian life.

Reform Act: lowers the minimum voting age for women from 21 years to 18.

Prince Charles is invested as Prince of Wales in Caernarvon, Wales.

Foundation of the Booker Prize for Fiction.

1970

✝ DEATHS   E M Forster: English novelist, author of *A Room with a View* and *Howards End*.

1971

✝ DEATHS   Stevie Smith: English poet and novelist.

★ EVENTS   Foundation of the Democratic Unionist Party: the
political party formed in Northern Ireland under the
leadership of Reverend Ian Paisley after a split in the Unionist
Party over Protestant reaction to demands both by Catholics
in the Province and from Westminster for greater social and
political equality. It has strong appeal to many working-class
Protestants and during the 1980s attracts about one-third of
the Unionist vote.

1972

✝ DEATHS   Edward VIII: King of the United Kingdom, son of
George V. Acceded to the throne in 1936 and abdicated the
same year after his proposal to the American divorcee, Wallis
Simpson.

★ EVENTS   'Bloody Sunday': 13 Northern Irish Catholics are
killed by British troops during a Catholic civil rights protest
march in Londonderry; leads to direct increase in support for
the IRA, the termination of the Stormont parliament and
British imposition of direct rule over Northern Ireland.

1973

✝ DEATHS   Robert Alexander Watson-Watt: Scottish physicist
and inventor of 'Radio Detection and Ranging', or RADAR.

Noel Coward: English actor, playwright and composer.

★ EVENTS   IRA restart terrorist campaign on the British
mainland.

The United Kingdom, Denmark and Ireland join the European
Economic Community (EEC).

1974

★ EVENTS   In the general election, the Scottish National Party
takes nearly a third of Scottish votes and wins 11 seats.

1975

✝ DEATHS   Eamon De Valera: Irish statesman and leader of the
Irish Volunteers in the 1916 Easter Rising.

1976

✝ DEATHS   Agatha Christie: English mystery writer, author of
more than 70 detective novels featuring either Hercules Poirot
or Miss Marple. Her play, *The Mouse Trap*, holds the record
for the longest run in theatre.

Montgomery of Alamein: British field marshal, commander of
the British North-Africa campaign.

Sir Basil Spence: Scottish architect, designer of the new
Coventry Cathedral and best known for his merging of new
and traditional structural methods.

Benjamin Britten: English composer, famed for his vocal and
choral works, and founder of the Aldeburgh Festival.

L S Lowry: English artist. From the 1920s he produced many
pictures of the Lancashire industrial scene, mainly in brilliant
whites and greys, peopled with scurrying 'matchstick' men
and women.

★ EVENTS   Introduction into regular service of Concorde.
Travelling at speeds of up to 1,200 miles per hour, Concorde
is the first supersonic, passenger-carrying aircraft to enter
commercial service.

1977

✝ DEATHS   Charlie Chaplin: English film actor and director,
whose hallmark was the bowler hat and cane adopted in his
early silent films.

Anthony Eden: Anglo-Irish politician and Prime Minister.

★ EVENTS   Rhodesia Crisis: Prime Minister Ian Smith
announces that he is willing to enter into new talks with the
Rhodesian government on a one-man, one-vote basis, and
releases nationalist leaders Ndabaningi Sithole and Joshua
Nkomo as a sign of good faith. However, they initially refuse
to participate in negotiations, and the escalation of terrorist
activities continues unabated despite Smith attaining an
internal settlement in 1978, thus providing for multiracial

government. The return of a Conservative Government in 1979 provides the springboard for fresh talks and a new settlement, leading to elections in 1980 that are won by the former Marxist guerrilla leader, Robert Mugabe.

Nationalization of the shipbuilding industry.

1978

✝ DEATHS   Hugh MacDiarmid (pseudonym of Christopher Murray Grieve): Scottish poet. As a member of the movement known as the Scottish Renaissance, he dedicated his work to the regeneration of the Scots language. Best known for *A Drunk Man Looks at the Thistle*.

1979

✝ DEATHS   Prince Louis Albert of Battenburg, later Louis Mountbatten, great-grandson of Queen Victoria: British Admiral of the Fleet and statesman. Killed by an IRA bomb while sailing near his holiday home in Ireland.

★ EVENTS   Margaret Thatcher becomes first female Prime Minister of Britain as the Conservative party seizes power from Labour.

Referendums oppose the proposed devolution of Scotland and of Wales.

1980

✝ DEATHS   Graham Sutherland: English artist. Official war artist (1941–5). He painted a controversial portrait of Winston Churchill which Lady Churchill had destroyed.

★ EVENTS   Over two million people in Britain are unemployed, reflecting, along with rocketing inflation rates, the depth of the recession.

The *Alexander Kielland*, a North Sea oil rig, collapses during a storm, causing the deaths of 100 oil workers.

20 hostages are seized at the Iranian Embassy in London, but are freed five days later after the building is stormed by the SAS.

1981

☦ DEATHS   Alfred Hitchcock: English film director.

✯ EVENTS   Margaret Thatcher and the Conservative party take radical measures to control the economy, attempting to reduce inflation and the interest rate at the cost of even higher unemployment. As a result, Thatcher is polled as possibly the most unpopular Prime Minister ever.

IRA hunger strikes in Northern Ireland lead to nine deaths and riots.

Social unrest results in rioting in Toxteth (Liverpool), Moss Side (Manchester) and Wood Green (London).

Foundation of the Social Democratic Party (SDP): formed by the 'Gang of Four', comprising David Owen, Shirley Williams, Roy Jenkins, and Bill Rogers. They break away from the Labour Party primarily over disagreements on policy and the degree of influence exerted on party policy by trade unions. Although espousing socialist principles, the party is a moderate centrist one. The SDP forms an electoral pact with the Liberals in 1981, but despite some early electoral successes fails to break the two-party 'mould' of British politics.

The construction of the Humber Bridge (begun 1973), the longest single-span suspension bridge in the world, over the River Humber, north-east England, is completed.

Beginning of unrest amongst British miners following the National Coal Board's announcement that it plans to close 50 pits.

After the death of a ninth IRA hunger striker, riots break out in Northern Ireland. When the Maze Prison hunger strikes end, 10 prisoners have died.

1982

☦ DEATHS   Sir John Charnley: British orthopaedic surgeon. He developed the technology and surgical techniques in the 1950s and 1960s for the replacement of arthritic hip joints.

✯ EVENTS   (2 Apr–14 Jun 1982) Falklands War: a war between Britain and Argentina, precipitated by the Argentine invasion of the Falkland Islands (known to Argentineans as the

Malvinas). Britain has ruled the islands continuously since 1833, but Argentina claims them by inheritance from the Spanish Empire and through their proximity to her shores. The British have been conducting talks with Argentina on sovereignty over the Falklands, involving either a leaseback arrangement or a joint administration. When these talks break down, the government of General Galtieri issues a warning to the British. The British government announces the withdrawal of HMS *Endurance* from the South Atlantic, and on 19 March scrap merchants land on South Georgia, ostensibly to demolish a whaling station, but they also raise the Argentine flag. On the night of 1–2 April the full-scale invasion of the Falklands begins. The British immediately send a task force to retake the islands. On 2 May the Argentine cruiser, *General Belgrano*, is sunk by the nuclear submarine, HMS *Conqueror*. South Georgia is retaken (25 Apr); the destroyer HMS *Sheffield* is sunk by an Exocet missile (4 May). The British forces take Darwin and Goose Green on 28 May, and after the recapture of the capital, Port Stanley, the Argentineans surrender (14 Jun). The war costs the British £700m; 254 British and 750 Argentine lives are lost; but some political commentators claim that it does much to save the declining fortunes of the government of Margaret Thatcher.

Bombing of Hyde Park in London by the IRA kills 12 and injures 50.

Remains of Henry VIII's warship, *Mary Rose*, are salvaged from the seabed and exhibited at Plymouth.

The first raising of the Thames barrier, designed to safeguard London from flooding.

Kielder Water, a reservoir in Northumberland, north-east England (built 1974–82 by damming the North Tyne River) becomes the first regional water grid system in the UK.

1983

✝ DEATHS Anthony Blunt: British double agent, art historian and Surveyor of the Queen's Pictures.

✮ EVENTS Landslide victory for the Conservatives in General Election, with a total collapse of Labour's vote.

Women peace campaigners force entry into Greenham Common
after the arrival of the first Cruise missiles.

IRA bombing of Harrods kills six people.

1984

✝ **DEATHS**   John Betjeman: English poet and broadcaster, Poet
Laureate from 1972. He despised modern architecture and
town planning.

✷ **EVENTS**   Following the announcement by the Coal Board of
the closure of 21 pits, the miners' strike begins.

A siege at the Libyan Embassy in London results in the death of
a female police officer and suspension of diplomatic links
between Britain and Libya. The siege ends and 30 Libyans
are deported.

The IRA bomb the Grand Hotel in Brighton during the
Conservative Party conference; four people die.

The future of Hong Kong is decided by an agreement which
states that it will revert from British control to Chinese in
1997.

Privatization of British Telecom.

1985

✝ **DEATHS**   Philip Larkin: English poet and novelist.

✷ **EVENTS**   Anglo-Irish Agreement: a joint agreement allowing
the Irish Republic to contribute to policy in Northern Ireland
for the first time since 1922, signed (15 Nov) by the British
and Irish Prime Ministers, Margaret Thatcher and Garrett
Fitzgerald. It establishes an intergovernmental conference to
discuss political, security, and legal matters affecting
Northern Ireland; early meetings focus on border co-
operation. Both governments pledge not to change the status
of Northern Ireland without the consent of the majority. The
agreement is opposed by the Irish Republic's opposition
party, Fianna Fáil; in Northern Ireland, Unionist leaders
withdraw co-operation with ministers and boycott official
bodies.

Ordination of women approved by the General synod of the
Church of England amidst strong opposition.

A Boeing 737 parked on the runway at Manchester airport
bursts into flames killing 54 people.

A fire at Bradford City Football Club kills 56 people.

Riots in Brixton and Broadwater Farm estates.

Discovery of the wreck of the *Titanic*.

1986

✝ DEATHS   Harold Macmillan: English politician.

Henry Moore: English sculptor. He produced mainly figures
and groups in a semi-abstract style.

✮ EVENTS   John McCarthy, English journalist, is abducted in
Lebanon by the revolutionary fundamentalist group, Islamic
Jihad. He is held hostage until Aug 1991.

Corporal punishment abolished in state schools.

Australia becomes fully independent from Britain.

Following the Chernobyl nuclear disaster in the USSR, Britain
fears possible radioactive fallout.

Passage of the Single European Act, allowing for the completion
of the process of creating a common market within the
community by the beginning of 1993.

Completion of the M25, the London orbital route.

A directive issued by the European Community concerning the
decline in demand for the building of new ships results in the
closure of many British shipyards.

Privatization of British Gas.

1987

✮ EVENTS   The Conservative party under Margaret Thatcher
comes to power for its third term, its success due to its
strength in the South and Midlands. The North–South divide
is emphasized by the fact that the Conservatives win only 10
seats in Scotland, which is generally hostile to them.

The Archbishop of Canterbury's special envoy Terry Waite is
taken hostage in Beirut during a mission to negotiate the
release of other hostages.

Capsize of the ferry the *Herald of Free Enterprise* outside
Zeebrugge harbour; 193 passengers and crew drown. The

subsequent enquiry finds that the deaths were unlawful and caused by overcrowding and lax security measures.

The worst hurricane to hit Britain since 1703 strikes, destroying 15 million trees and killing 17 people.

Bomb explosion on Remembrance day in Enniskillen, Northern Ireland, kills 11 people.

Michael Ryan shoots 16 people dead in the Berkshire village of Hungerford.

A fire in the King's Cross tube station results in the deaths of 31 people; smoking in the Underground system is subsequently banned.

Privatization of British Airways.

1988

✝ DEATHS   Kim Philby: British double agent.

★ EVENTS   Margaret Thatcher becomes the longest serving Prime Minister of the century.

Explosion on the Piper Alpha oil rig in the North Sea leads to the deaths of 150 oil workers.

Terrorist bombing of a Pan-Am jumbo jet over Scottish town of Lockerbie results in the deaths of 281 people.

Merger of the Social Democratic Party with the Liberal Party to create the Social and Liberal Democratic Party.

Edwina Currie, junior health minister, bows to public pressure and resigns following her comments that most eggs produced in Britain are infected with salmonella.

34 die when two trains collide at Clapham Junction.

Privatization of British Steel.

1989

✝ DEATHS   Samuel Beckett: Irish novelist, poet and playwright, best known for his groundbreaking play *Waiting for Godot*.

Daphne du Maurier: English novelist, best known for *Rebecca*.

Laurence Olivier: English actor, producer and director.

★ EVENTS   Widespread opposition in Scotland to the introduction of the Community Charge (Poll Tax).

A Boeing 737 crashes onto the M1 motorway near the Midlands town of Kegworth, Leicestershire, killing 47 people.

The worst disaster in British sporting history occurs at the FA Cup semi-final match between Liverpool and Nottingham Forest at Hillsborough Stadium in Sheffield. Owing mainly to crushing at the perimeter fences, 95 Liverpool fans die and 400 others are injured.

Parliament agrees to the privatization of the water and electricity industries. Britain's nuclear power stations remain in public ownership.

Author Salman Rushdie goes into hiding following the issue of a *fatwa* (death sentence) against him by the Iranian leader over alleged blasphemy in *The Satanic Verses*.

1990

✟ DEATHS   Roald Dahl: British writer. He specialized in writing short stories of unexpected horror and macabre surprise, and children's books displaying a similar taste for the grotesque.

✯ EVENTS   Widespread demonstrations in England against the Community Charge (Poll Tax).

Inmates of Strangeways Prison riot and seize the prison for 25 days.

Conservative leadership contest results in the ousting of Margaret Thatcher and her replacement with John Major, who defeats the other candidates Michael Heseltine and Douglas Hurd.

End of the Cold War: a process of detente to diffuse the state of tension and hostility between the Soviet Union and the major Western non-communist states, begun in the late 1960s, leads through two decades of arms reduction and control negotiations to the 'end' of the Cold War. Mainly as a result of a dramatic change in the Soviet attitude under Mikhail Gorbachev.

RULERS OF ENGLAND
(dating from the first 'King of the English')

779–96	Offa	1272–1307	Edward I
802–39	Egbert	1307–27	Edward II
839–56	Ethelwulf	1327–77	Edward III
856–60	Ethelbald	1377–99	Richard II
860–5	Ethelbert	1399–1413	Henry IV
865–71	Ethelred I	1413–22	Henry V
871–99	Alfred the Great	1422–61	Henry VI
899–924	Edward the Elder	1461–83	Edward IV
924–39	Athelstan	1483	Edward V
939–46	Edmund	1483–5	Richard III
946–55	Edred	1485–1509	Henry VII
955–9	Edwy	1509–47	Henry VIII
959–75	Edgar	1547–53	Edward VI
975–8	Edward the Martyr	1553–8	Mary I
978–1016	Ethelred II, the Unready	1558–1603	Elizabeth I
1016	Edmund Ironside	1603–25	James I (King of Scotland as James VI 1567–1625)
1016–35	Canute		
1035–40	Harold I Harefoot	1625–49	Charles I
1040–2	Hardicanute	1649–53	Commonwealth
1042–66	Edward the Confessor	1653–8	Oliver Cromwell (Lord Protector)
1066	Harold II		
1066–87	William I	1658–9	Richard Cromwell (Lord Protector)
1087–1100	William II		
1100–35	Henry I	1660–85	Charles II
1135–54	Stephen	1685–8	James II (King of Scotland as James VII)
1154–89	Henry II		
1189–99	Richard I	1689–94	William III and Mary II (jointly)
1199–1216	John		
1216–72	Henry III	1694–1702	William III (alone)

RULERS OF SCOTLAND
(dating from the first king of the united
Scots of Dalriada and the Picts)

843–58	Kenneth I (MacAlpin)	1107–24	Alexander I
858–62	Donald I	1124–53	David I
862–77	Constantine I	1153–65	Malcolm IV, 'the Maiden'
877–8	Aed	1165–1214	William I, 'the Lion'
878–89	Giric and Eochaid	1214–49	Alexander II
889–900	Donald II	1249–86	Alexander III
900–43	Constantine II	1286–90	Margaret ('Maid of
943–54	Malcolm I		Norway')
954–62	Indulf	1290–2	Interregnum
962–6	Dubh	1292–6	John Balliol
966–71	Culen	1296–1306	Interregnum
971–95	Kenneth II	1306–29	Robert I, 'the Bruce'
995–7	Constantine III	1329–71	David II
c.997–1005	Kenneth III (and Giric?)	1371–90	Robert II
1005–34	Malcolm II	1390–1406	Robert III
1034–40	Duncan I	1406–37	James I
1040–57	Macbeth	1437–60	James II
1057–8	Lulach	1460–88	James III
1058–93	Malcolm III, 'Canmore'	1488–1513	James IV
1093–4	Donald III (Donald Bane)	1513–42	James V
1094	Duncan II	1542–67	Mary, Queen of Scots
1094–7	Donald III (Donald Bane)	1567–1625	James VI
1097–1107	Edgar		

MONARCHS OF GREAT BRITAIN AND IRELAND

1702–14	Anne
1714–27	George I
1727–60	George II
1760–1820	George III (Elector, 1760–1815, and King, 1815–20, of Hanover)
1820–30	George IV
1830–7	William IV (King of Hanover 1830–7)
1837–1901	Victoria (Empress of India 1876–1901)
1901–10	Edward VII
1910–36	George V
1936	Edward VIII
1936–52	George VI
1952–	Elizabeth II (Head of the Commonwealth of Nations)

RULING DYNASTIES

827–1016	Saxons
1016–42	Danes
1042–66	Saxons
1066–1135	House of Normandy
1135–54	House of Blois
1154–1399	House of Plantagenet
1399–1461	House of Lancaster
1461–85	House of York
1485–1603	House of Tudor
1603–1714	House of Stuart (except the years between 1649 and 1660)
1714–1901	House of Hanover
1901–10	House of Saxe-Coburg-Gotha
1910–	House of Windsor

MAJOR WARS AND BATTLES

c.55 BC	Roman Conquest of Britain begins
c.61 AD	Boudicca leads revolt against the Romans
AD 84	Defeat of the British at Mons Graupius
367	Attack by Picts, Scots and Saxons on Romans in Britain
c.409	Beginning of Saxon raids
515	Battle of Mount Badon
577	Battle of Dyrham
591	Battle at Adam's Grave
607	Battle at Chester
632	Northumbrian army defeated at Hatfield
654	Battle of Winwaed
685	Battle of Nectansmere
787	First recorded raid by the Danes
795	Norse attack on Ireland
c.800–c.1042	Viking raids. 856–875: first full Viking onslaught. 892–9: fresh armies. 980: Viking raids recommence. 991: Sweyn I Forkbeard of Denmark leads yet another onset.
1014	Brian of Munster defeats the Norse at Clontarf
1066	Battles of Stamford Bridge and Hastings
1095–9	First Crusade
1106	Battle of Tinchebrai
1109–13	War between England and France
1135	Stephen of Blois seizes English crown: civil war breaks out
1138	Battle of the Standard
1141	Battle of Lincoln
1147–9	Second Crusade
1153	Henry of Anjou invades England
1189–92	Third Crusade
1202–4	Fourth Crusade
1224–7	Anglo-French war
1277–82	Edward I embarks on successful conquest of Wales
1297	Battle of Cambuskenneth
1298	Battle of Falkirk
1314	Battle of Bannockburn
1337–1453	Hundred Years War. 1340: Battle of Sluys. 1346: Battle of Crécy. 1356: Battle of Poitiers. 1415: Battle of Agincourt.
1403	Battle of Shrewsbury
1429	Siege of Orléans
1455–85	Wars of the Roses. 1455: Battle of St Albans. 1461: Second Battle of St Albans. 1485: Battle of Bosworth Field.
1513	Battle of Flodden
1513	Battle of the Spurs
1542	Battle of Solway Moss
1544	Henry VIII and Charles V invade France
1547	Battle of Pinkie
1558	England loses Calais
1587	England wars with Spain
1588	Defeat of Spanish Armada
1639–40	The Bishops Wars. 1639: First Bishops War. 1640: Second Bishops War.
1641–9	Great Irish Rebellion
1642–6	First English Civil War. 1642: Battle of Edgehill.

213

Major Wars and Battles

1642–6 (contd)	1643: Battles of Newbury and Lostwithiel. 1644: Battle of Marston Moor, Second Battle of Newbury. 1645: Battles of Inverlochy, Naseby and Philiphaugh.	1775–83	American War of Independence. 1775: Battles of Lexington and Concord and Bunker Hill. 1776: Battle of Long Island. 1777: Battles of Saratoga and Brandywine Creek. 1778: Battle of Monmouth. 1780: Battles of Camden and Charleston. 1781: Battle of Cowpens and Yorktown Campaign. 1782: Battle of the Saintes.
1646	Surrender of Charles I at Battle of Newark		
1648	Second English Civil War: Battle of Preston		
1650	Battle of Dunbar		
1651	Battle of Worcester		
1652–74	Three wars between England and Dutch Republic: 1652–4, 1664–7 and 1672–4.	1794	Battle of the Glorious First of June
		1797	Battles of Cape St Vincent and Camperdown
1666	Battle of Pentland Hills	1798	Battle of Aboukir Bay
1679	Battle of Bothwell Bridge	1805	Battle of Trafalgar
1685	Battle of Sedgemoor	1808–14	Peninsular War. 1809: Battle of Corunna.
1689	Battle of Killiecrankie		
1689–95	King William's War, also known as War of the League of Augsburg	1812–14	War of 1812
		1815	Battle of Waterloo
1690	Battle of the Boyne	1854–6	Crimean War
1692	Battle of La Hogue	1880–1	First Boer War.
1702–13	War of the Spanish Succession	1899–1902	Second Boer War. 1900: Battles of Ladysmith and Mafeking.
1704	Battle of Blenheim		
1715–16	Jacobite Rebellion. 1715: Battle of Sherriffmuir.	1914–18	World War I. 1914: Battles of Liège, Marne, Ypres and Mons. 1915: Second battle of Ypres, battles of Neuve Chapelle, Artois, Champagne and Loos. Dardanelles and Gallipoli campaigns. 1916: Battles of the Somme, Jutland and Verdun. 1917: Third battle of Ypres. 1918: Battles of Amiens and Antwerp.
1727–9	War of England and France against Spain		
1739	War of Jenkins' Ear, becomes the War of Austrian Succession		
1743	Battle of Dettingen		
1745–6	Jacobite Rebellion. 1745: Battle of Prestonpans. 1746: Battle of Culloden.		
1756–63	Seven Years War		
1759	Battle of Quebec	1920	Civil War in Ireland
1762	Britain declares war on Spain	1939–45	World War II. 1940: Evacuation of Dunkirk and

1939–45 (contd)	Battles of Britain and Flanders. 1942: Battle of El Alamein. 1944: D-Day. 1945: Bombings of		Dresden, Hiroshima and Nagasaki.
		1982	Falklands War
		1991	Gulf War

PRIME MINISTERS OF GREAT BRITAIN

1721–42	Robert Walpole *Whig*
1742–3	Earl of Wilmington (Spencer Compton) *Whig*
1743–54	Henry Pelham *Whig*
1754–6	Duke of Newcastle (Thomas Pelham-Holles) *Whig*
1756–7	Duke of Devonshire (William Cavendish) *Whig*
1757–62	Duke of Newcastle *Whig*
1762–3	Earl of Bute (John Stuart) *Tory*
1763–5	George Grenville *Whig*
1765–6	Marquess of Rockingham (Charles Watson Wentworth) *Whig*
1766–70	Duke of Grafton (Augustus Henry Fitzroy) *Whig*
1770–82	Lord North (Frederick North) *Tory*
1782	Marquess of Rockingham *Whig*
1782–3	Earl of Shelburne (William Petty-Fitzmaurice) *Whig*
1783	Duke of Portland (William Henry Cavendish) *Coalition*
1783–1801	William Pitt (the Elder) *Tory*
1801–4	Henry Addington *Tory*
1804–6	William Pitt (the Younger) *Tory*
1806–7	Lord Grenville (William Wyndham) *Whig*
1807–9	Duke of Portland *Tory*
1809–12	Spencer Perceval *Tory*
1812–27	Earl of Liverpool (Robert Banks Jenkinson) *Tory*
1827	George Canning *Tory*
1827–8	Viscount Goderich (Frederick John Robinson) *Tory*

1828–30	Duke of Wellington (Arthur Wellesley) *Tory*
1830–4	Earl Grey (Charles Grey) *Whig*
1834	Viscount Melbourne (William Lamb) *Whig*
1834–5	Robert Peel *Conservative*
1835–41	Viscount Melbourne *Whig*
1841–6	Robert Peel *Conservative*
1846–52	Lord John Russell *Liberal*
1852	Earl of Derby (Edward George Stanley) *Conservative*
1852–5	Lord Aberdeen (George Hamilton-Gordon) *Peelite*
1855–8	Viscount Palmerston (Henry John Temple) *Liberal*
1858–9	Earl of Derby *Conservative*
1859–65	Viscount Palmerston *Liberal*
1865–6	Lord John Russell *Liberal*
1866–8	Earl of Derby *Conservative*
1868	Benjamin Disraeli *Conservative*
1868–74	William Ewart Gladstone *Liberal*
1874–80	Benjamin Disraeli *Conservative*
1880–5	William Ewart Gladstone *Liberal*
1885–6	Marquess of Salisbury (Robert Gascoyne-Cecil) *Conservative*
1886	William Ewart Gladstone *Liberal*
1886–92	Marquess of Salisbury *Conservative*
1892–4	William Ewart Gladstone *Liberal*

1894–5	Earl of Rosebery (Archibald Philip Primrose) *Liberal*	1931–5	James Ramsay MacDonald *Nationalist*
1895–1902	Marquess of Salisbury *Conservative*	1935–7	Stanley Baldwin *Nationalist*
1902–5	Arthur James Balfour *Conservative*	1937–40	Arthur Neville Chamberlain *Nationalist*
1905–8	Henry Campbell-Bannerman *Liberal*	1940–5	Winston Churchill *Coalition*
1908–15	Herbert Henry Asquith *Liberal*	1945–51	Clement Attlee *Labour*
1915–16	Herbert Henry Asquith *Coalition*	1951–5	Winston Churchill *Conservative*
1916–22	David Lloyd George *Coalition*	1955–7	Anthony Eden *Conservative*
1922–3	Andrew Bonar Law *Conservative*	1957–63	Harold Macmillan *Conservative*
1923–4	Stanley Baldwin *Conservative*	1963–4	Alec Douglas-Home *Conservative*
1924	James Ramsay MacDonald *Labour*	1964–70	Harold Wilson *Labour*
1924–9	Stanley Baldwin *Conservative*	1970–4	Edward Heath *Conservative*
1929–31	James Ramsay MacDonald *Labour*	1974–6	Harold Wilson *Labour*
		1976–9	James Callaghan *Labour*
		1979–90	Margaret Thatcher *Conservative*
		1990–	John Major *Conservative*

Founding Dates of British Universities

FOUNDING DATES OF BRITISH UNIVERSITIES

1249	University College, Oxford
1263	Balliol College, Oxford
1264	Merton College, Oxford
1278	St Edmund Hall, Oxford
1284	Peterhouse College, Cambridge
1314	Exeter College, Oxford
1326	Clare College, Cambridge
	Oriel College, Oxford
1340	Queen's College, Oxford
1347	Pembroke College, Cambridge
1348	Gonville College, Cambridge (refounded as Gonville and Caius, 1558)
1350	Trinity Hall, Cambridge
1352	Corpus Christi College, Cambridge
1379	New College, Oxford
1411	University of St Andrews
1427	Lincoln College, Oxford
1438	All Souls College, Oxford
1441	King's College, Cambridge
1448	Queen's College, Cambridge
1451	University of Glasgow
1458	Magdalen College, Oxford
1473	St Catharine's College, Cambridge
1495	University of Aberdeen
1496	Jesus College, Cambridge
1505	Christ's College, Cambridge
1509	Brasenose College, Oxford
1511	St John's College, Cambridge
1517	Corpus Christi College, Oxford
1542	Magdalene College, Cambridge
1546	Trinity College, Cambridge
	Christ Church College, Oxford
1554	Trinity College, Oxford
1555	St John's College, Oxford
1571	Jesus College, Oxford
1583	University of Edinburgh
1584	Emmanuel College, Cambridge
1596	Sidney Sussex College, Cambridge
1612	Wadham College, Oxford
1624	Pembroke College, Oxford
1714	Worcester College, Oxford
1800	Downing College, Cambridge
1810	Regent's Park College, Oxford
1824	University of Manchester Institute of Science and Technology
	Homerton College, Cambridge
1832	University of Durham (reorganized 1908/1937/1963)
1836	University of London
1837	Royal College Of Art
1851	University of Manchester (reorganized 1880/1903)
1852	University of Newcastle upon Tyne (reorganized 1908/1937/1963)
1868	Keble College, Oxford
1869	Girton College, Cambridge
1871	Newnham College, Cambridge
1874	Hertford College, Oxford
1878	Lady Margaret Hall, Oxford
1879	Somerville College, Oxford
1882	Selwyn College, Cambridge
1885	Hughes Hall, Cambridge
1886	Mansfield College, Oxford
	St Hugh's College, Oxford
1893	St Hilda's College, Oxford
	University of Wales
1896	St Edmund's College, Cambridge
	Campion Hall, Oxford
1897	St Benet's Hall, Oxford
1900	University of Birmingham
1903	University of Liverpool
1904	University of Leeds
1905	University of Sheffield
1908	Queen's University of Belfast
1909	University of Bristol
1910	Greyfriars College, Oxford
1926	University of Reading

1929	St Peter's College, Oxford
1937	Nuffield College, Oxford
1948	University of Nottingham
1950	St Anthony's College, Oxford
1952	University of Southampton
	St Anne's College, Oxford
1954	University of Hull
	New Hall, Cambridge
1955	University of Exeter
1957	University of Leicester
1960	Churchill College, Cambridge
1961	University of Sussex
1962	University of Keele
	Linacre College, Oxford
	St Catherine's College, Oxford
1963	University of East Anglia
	University of York
1964	University of Lancaster
	Lucy Cavendish College, Cambridge
	Darwin College, Cambridge
	University of Strathclyde
	University of Essex
1965	University of Warwick
	University of Kent at Canterbury
	Wolfson College, Cambridge
	St Cross College, Oxford
1966	City University
	Brunel University
	University of Bradford
	University of Bath
	Aston University
	Clare Hall, Cambridge
	Fitzwilliam College, Cambridge
	Wolfson College, Oxford
	Heriot-Watt University
	Loughborough University of Technology
	University of Surrey
1967	University of Stirling
	University of Dundee
	University of Salford

1969	Open University
	Cranfield University
1977	Robinson College, Cambridge
1979	Green College, Oxford
1983	University of Buckingham
1984	University of Ulster
1990	Rewley House College, Oxford
	Manchester House, Oxford
1992	Liverpool John Moores University
	Leeds Metropolitan University
	Kingston University
	University of Humberside
	University of Huddersfield
	University of Hertfordshire
	Anglia Polytechnic University
	Bournemouth University
	University of Brighton
	University of Central England in Birmingham
	University of Central Lancashire
	Coventry University
	De Montfort University
	University of East London
	Glamorgan University
	University of Greenwich
	Napier University
	Middlesex University
	Manchester Metropolitan University
	University of North London
	University of Northumbria at Newcastle
	University of Paisley
	Nottingham Trent University
	University of Plymouth
	University of Portsmouth
	Robert Gordon University
	South Bank University
	Sheffield Hallam University
	University of Sunderland
	Staffordshire University
	University of Teesside

Founding Dates of British Universities

1992 (contd)	Thames Valley University	1993	University of Derby
	University of Westminster		Glasgow Caledonian University
	University of Wolverhampton		London Guildhall University
	University of the West of England, Bristol		University of Luton
			Oxford Brookes University

	GREAT EXPLORATIONS
1497	Exploring under letters of patent from Henry VII, John Cabot sights land (probably Cape Breton Island, Novia Scotia) and claims North America for England
1526	Sebastian Cabot explores the coast of South America for Charles V
1572	Francis Drake becomes the first Englishman to see the Pacific Ocean
1577–80	Francis Drake is the first Englishman to circumnavigate the world
1584–9	Walter Raleigh sends an expedition to America to take unknown lands in the name of Elizabeth I; although his attempts to colonize Virginia are unsuccessful, he does successfully introduce tobacco and potatoes into Britain
1595	Walter Raleigh explores the coasts of Trinidad and sails up the Orinoco
1607–9	Henry Hudson sails in search of a passage across the North Pole (1607), reaches Novaya Zemlya (1608), and discovers the Hudson River (1609)
1616	William Baffin discovers Baffin Bay
1620	The Pilgrim Fathers establish Plymouth Colony in America
1699	William Dampier leads a voyage of discovery to the South Seas, where he explores the NW coast of Australia, and gives his name to the Dampier Archipelago and Strait
1769–70	James Cook circumnavigates New Zealand and charts part of Australia
1772–5	James Cook sails round Antarctica and discovers several Pacific island groups
1776–9	Third voyage of James Cook, on which he aims to discover a passage round the north coast of America from the Pacific, but is forced to turn back, and on his return journey is killed by natives on Hawaii
1795	George Vancouver sails round the island on the west coast of North America later named after him
1796–7	Mungo Park explores the River Niger, and the direction of its flow is at last determined
1828–45	Charles Sturt heads three important expeditions; he discovers the Darling (1828) and the lower Murray (1830)
1831	James Ross discovers the north magnetic pole
1839–43	An expedition by James Ross to the Antarctic seas results in the discovery of the Ross Barrier, the Ross Sea, and Ross Island
1840	Edward Eyre explores part of the region between South and West Australia, and discovers Lake Eyre
1845–7	John Franklin commands an expedition to discover the Northwest Passage; both he and his crew die, but he is credited with the discovery

Great Explorations

1852–6	David Livingstone travels north of Bechuanaland (now Botswana) and discovers Lake Ngami and the Victoria Falls
1858–63	David Livingstone leads an expedition to the Zambezi and discovers Lake Shirwa and Lake Nyasa
1858	Richard Francis Burton and John Hanning Speke discover Lake Tanganyika; travelling on alone Speke finds the lake which he names Victoria, and identifies as the source of the Nile
1860	Burke and Wills expedition across the Australian continent from south to north
1860	John Hanning Speke returns to the Victoria Nyanza with James Grant; they track the Nile flowing out of it, in retaliation against the doubts of Richard Francis Burton and others
1874	Henry Stanley leads his second expedition to explore Lake Tanganyika, and traces the Congo to the sea
1886	Francis Younghusband explores Manchuria and discovers the route from Kashgar into India via the Mustagh Pass
1901–4	Robert Falcon Scott commands the National Antarctic Expedition, which explores the Ross Sea area, and discovers King Edward VII Land
1910–12	Robert Falcon Scott's second expedition to the South Pole is beaten by the Norwegian expedition by one month; all members of the party die
1930–2	Amy Johnson flies solo from England to Australia in nine and a half days (1930), then to Japan via Siberia (1931) and to Cape Town, South Africa (1932), making new records in each case
1957–8	Vivian Fuchs, leading the British Commonwealth Trans-Antarctic Expedition, makes an overland crossing from Shackleton Base via the South Pole to Scott Base
1979–82	Ranulph Fiennes organizes the Transglobe expedition which traces the Greenwich Meridian across both Poles
1993	Ranulph Fiennes and Michael Stroud successfully complete the first-ever unsupported crossing of the Antarctic on foot

DISCOVERIES AND INVENTIONS

The Sixteenth Century

William Gilbert (1544–1603) He was the first to propose that the Earth behaves like one vast bar magnet linking the North and South Poles

John Harrington (1561–1612) His epigram, *The Metamorphosis of Ajax*, contained the earliest design for a water closet

The Seventeenth Century

Robert Boyle (1627–91) He founded the study of chemistry as a separate science, and formulated Boyle's Law (1662), which states that the volume of a gas at a constant temperature varies inversely with the pressure applied to the gas

James Gregory (1638–75) He invented the Gregorian reflecting telescope in 1661

William Harvey (1578–1657) He provided the first accurate description of the circulation of the blood, in a treatise published in 1628, and he proposed that the heart functions as a pump

Robert Hooke (1635–1703) His research on the elastic behaviour of springs led him to develop Hooke's law, which states that the extent to which an elastic body is deformed is directly proportional to the force acting on it. He also invented the spirit level, a marine barometer, and the 'universal joint', which is used to change the direction of a rotating shaft

John Napier (1550–1617) In 1614 he invented logarithms for the purpose of simplifying calculations. He also devised an early calculating machine, using a set of rods, known as 'Napier's bones'

Isaac Newton (1642–1727) He discovered the laws of mechanics and the law of gravity, explained the orbits of the planets around the Sun, constructed the first reflecting telescope and developed the mathematical techniques of calculus. He also demonstrated that white light is composed of many different colours

Thomas Savery (c.1650–1715) In 1696 he invented the steam-driven water pump, which eventually led to the development of the steam engine

Discoveries and Inventions

The Eighteenth Century

Richard Arkwright (1732–92)	He invented a water-powered spinning machine, known as Arkwright's water frame (1767)
Joseph Black (1728–99)	In 1754 he discovered carbon dioxide
Edmund Cartwright (1743–1823)	He patented the first power loom in 1785, and the first wool-combing machine in 1789
Henry Cavendish (1731–1810)	He discovered the properties of hydrogen, which he called 'inflammable air', in 1766, and he showed that air is a mixture of more than one gas. He was also the first to show that water is a compound and not an element
Abraham Darby (c.1678–1717)	He was the first to smelt iron ore with coke instead of charcoal, enabling iron to be produced more cheaply
Edmond Halley (1656–1742)	He correctly predicted that a comet observed in 1682, now named after him, would return in 1758
James Hargreaves (c.1720–78)	About 1764 he invented the spinning-jenny, a hand-driven spinning machine that enabled a number of threads to be spun simultaneously
Edward Jenner (1749–1823)	He pioneered the use of vaccination to confer temporary or permanent immunity to a bacterial or viral disease, and in 1796 he performed the first successful inoculations against disease, based on his observation that inoculation with cowpox gives people immunity to smallpox
John Kay (1704–c.1780)	In 1733 he patented his flying shuttle, a machine designed to increase the speed of hand-loom weaving and to increase the width of cloth that could be woven
James Lind (1716–94)	The results of his research on cures for and prevention of scurvy allowed the incidence of the disease within the navy to be substantially reduced
Thomas Newcomen (1663–1729)	In 1712 he built the first steam engine, used to pump water from coal mines
William Nicholson (1816–64)	He not only invented the hydrometer, but also a machine for printing on linen. In 1800, he discovered electrolysis
James Parkinson (1755–1824)	In 1817 he gave the first description of Parkinson's disease
Joseph Priestley (1733–1804)	In 1774 he discovered oxygen

Ernest Rutherford (1871–1937)	In 1911 he discovered the atomic nucleus, and he subsequently described many of its properties, so helping to lay the foundations of modern nuclear physics. He showed that there are different types of radioactivity, which he called alpha, beta, and gamma rays, and in 1919 he succeeded in splitting an atom
Benjamin Thompson Rumford (1753–1814)	He was the first to demonstrate the relationship between heat and work, a concept fundamental to modern physics, and in 1798 he proposed that heat represents the vibratory motion of atoms or molecules
Jethro Tull (1674–1740)	In 1701 he developed a mechanical seed drill that enabled seeds to be sown in rows spaced so that the soil between adjacent rows of plants could be easily cultivated
James Watt (1736–1819)	He greatly improved the efficiency of the steam engine, in 1764 incorporating a separate condenser which converted waste steam back to water. As a result of this work steam engines were established as a major source of power in factories in the 1780s, during the Industrial Revolution

The Nineteenth Century

George Biddell Airy (1801–92)	He was the first to make accurate measurements of Greenwich Mean Time, using a telescope at the Royal Observatory, Greenwich, UK, to observe the stars as they crossed the meridian
Charles Babbage (1791–1871)	He designed two mechanical calculating machines, known as the Difference Engine and the Analytical Engine. Although these devices were never completed, they operated on similar principles to present-day digital computers
Joseph William Bazalgette (1819–91)	He designed and supervised the construction of London's sewer system, which was completed in 1865, and he designed the Victoria Embankment
Alexander Graham Bell (1847–1922)	He perfected the telephone, and made the first telephone call on the New York to Chicago telephone line in 1892. He also invented the gramophone, which was an improved version of the phonograph, in 1880
Henry Bessemer (1813–98)	In 1855 he patented an economical process for the

	large-scale manufacture of steel, known as the Bessemer process, whereby air was blasted through molten pig iron to remove impurities
David Brewster (1781–1868)	He made important discoveries concerning the diffraction and polarization of light, and he invented the kaleidoscope in 1816
David Bruce (1855–1931)	In 1895 in South Africa he discovered that the tsetse fly was the carrier of the parasite responsible for sleeping sickness in humans and the disease nagana in cattle
Isambard Kingdom Brunel (1806–59)	He designed the Clifton Suspension Bridge over the river Avon in Bristol, and in 1883 he became chief engineer to the Great Western Railway, supervising the construction of over 1500km of railway. He also designed the *Great Western*, the first steamship to cross the Atlantic regularly, and the *Great Eastern*, until 1899 the largest vessel ever built
George Cayley (1773–1857)	In 1853 he constructed the first successful piloted glider, which travelled 270m. He also invented the biplane and the caterpillar tractor. He is often referred to as the father of modern aeronautics
John Dalton (1766–1844)	In 1808 he published an account of the atomic theory of matter, in which he proposed that chemical elements consist of atoms, and that atoms of different elements combine to form compounds
Charles Robert Darwin (1809–82)	He developed the modern theory of evolution, which he described in *The Origin of Species by Means of Natural Selection* (1859). In a second book, *The Descent of Man* (1871), he traced man's ancestors back to ape-like creatures
Humphry Davy (1778–1829)	He discovered that nitrous oxide (laughing gas) could be used as an anaesthetic, and he was the first to demonstrate that chemical compounds could be separated to their elements by passing an electric current through them. Using this process, known as electrolysis, he discovered the elements sodium and potassium in 1807, and calcium, boron, magnesium, strontium, and barium in 1808. In 1815, he invented the miner's safety lamp, designed to prevent the explosion of fire-damp during work in coal mines
James Dewar (1842–1923)	He invented the vacuum flask (also known as a Dewar

flask), and in 1891, together with Frederick Abel, he developed cordite, a smokeless propellant explosive for cartridges and shells

John Boyd Dunlop (1840–1921)	He developed the first commercially successful pneumatic tyres, and founded the rubber company that bears his name
William Friese-Greene (1855–1921)	In the 1880s he designed a camera to expose a sequence of photographs for projection as a moving image by lantern slides
William Robert Grove (1811–96)	He invented a 'gas battery' (the first fuel cell, 1842), and the earliest form of filament lamp intended for use in mines
Edmund Gurney (1847–88)	He conducted important experimental research on hypnosis and telepathy, and made a statistical survey of hallucinations
David Edward Hughes (1831–1900)	He invented a telegraph typewriter (1855), and a microphone and an induction balance (1878)
William Thomson Kelvin (1824–1907)	He introduced the absolute (Kelvin) scale of temperature, and his work on the conservation of energy contributed to the second law of thermodynamics, which states that heat cannot be completely converted into work. He also designed a galvanometer to receive the signals sent through underwater telegraph cables
John Bennet Lawes (1814–1900)	He developed the use of artificial fertilizers in agriculture, and in 1843 he established the first factory for the manufacture of such fertilizers
Joseph Lister (1827–1912)	He founded the practice of antiseptic surgery, which greatly reduced the incidence of post-operative deaths caused by bacterial infection. His system involved the sterilization of instruments by heat and the use of a solution of carbolic acid to clean wounds and surgical cuts, as well as antiseptic sprays to sterilize the air in operating theatres. He also devised new operations and invented several surgical instruments
Joseph Norman Lockyer (1836–1920)	In studies of the Sun he designed a spectroscope for observing prominences (1868), and in the same year he identified an unknown element which he named helium (the 'Sun element'), not detected on Earth until 1895

Discoveries and Inventions

William MacEwen (1848–1924)	He extended Joseph Lister's antiseptic surgical techniques, and pioneered operations on the brain for tumours, abscesses, and trauma; he also operated on bones, introducing methods of implanting small grafts to replace missing portions
James Mackenzie (1853–1925)	He developed a 'polygraph' for recording the pulse, and he investigated the heartbeat
Kirkpatrick MacMillan (1813–78)	In 1840 he built the first bicycle, but he never patented his invention and it was widely copied
Patrick Manson (1844–1922)	He was the first to propose that insects are responsible for the spread of various diseases, and in particular that the mosquito is host to the malaria parasite (1877)
Gideon Algernon Mantell (1790–1852)	He discovered several dinosaur types (1825)
Charles Algernon Parsons (1854–1931)	In 1884 he invented the first practical steam turbine, which subsequently replaced the steam engine in electrical power generators. He also developed the first turbine-driven steamship in 1897
James Simpson (1811–70)	In 1847 he introduced the use of chloroform as an anaesthetic during surgery and childbirth, and in the same year he was the first to use ether as an anaesthetic during childbirth
John Snow (1813–58)	He established that severe cholera outbreaks are caused by contaminated water supplies. He also devised apparatus to administer anaesthetics
Joseph Wilson Swan (1828–1914)	In 1860 he invented the incandescent-filament electric lamp or light bulb. He also invented a type of bromide paper which subsequently gave rise to the development of photographic film
William Henry Fox Talbot (1800–77)	In 1839 he invented the Calotype process, enabling many positive prints to be made from one transparent negative, and so laying the foundation for modern photographic processes. He was also the first to use 'flash photography' (1851)
Richard Trevithick (1771–1833)	He built the first steam road locomotive in 1801, and the first steam railway locomotive in 1804
Alfred Wallace (1823–1913)	He conceived the idea of natural selection as the key to evolution independently of and at around the same time as Charles Darwin

| Charles Wheatstone (1802–75) | Together with William Cooke he patented an electric telegraph in 1837, and he also invented a 'stereoscope' a device that produces an apparently three-dimensional image by presenting a slightly different view of the same object to each eye. In 1829 he invented the concertina. He did not invent the Wheatstone bridge, named after him, but he used it extensively |
| Joseph Whitworth (1803–87) | In 1859 he invented a gun of compressed steel, but he is best known as the inventor of extremely precise machine tools |

The Twentieth Century

Edgar Douglas Adrian (1889–1977)	He designed equipment to study the minute electrical impulses of nerves
John William Alcock (1892–1919)	With Arthur Whitten Brown he made the first non-stop flight across the Atlantic Ocean on 14 June 1919 in a Vickers–Vimy machine (16 hours 27 minutes)
Edward Victor Appleton (1892–1965)	He demonstrated the existence of one of the layers of electrically charged particles that reflect radio waves in the Earth's upper atmosphere. This layer was formerly known as the Appleton layer, but is now understood to be composed of two separate layers, known as F1 and F2. His research on atmospheric physics played an important part in the development of radar
John Logie Baird (1888–1946)	In 1925 he gave the first public demonstration of transmission of a television picture by radio waves. In 1928 he became the first person to transmit a television picture across the Atlantic, and in the same year he transmitted colour television pictures
James Black (1924–)	His research on heart disease led to the discovery of betablocker drugs (which reduce the heartbeat rate and decrease blood pressure) in 1964, and his proposals in 1972 regarding acid secretion in the stomach led to the development of anti-ulcer drugs
Hugh Cairns (1922–)	He demonstrated that cancer develops from a single abnormal cell, but that the further progression of a cancer is dependent on multiple environmental factors such as smoking, diet, and hormones

Discoveries and Inventions

Hugh Longbourne Callendar (1863–1930)	He devised a constant-pressure air thermometer which could measure temperatures of up to 450°C. He also developed an accurate platinum resistance thermometer
James Chadwick (1891–1974)	In 1932 he discovered that the nuclei of all atoms except those of hydrogen contain neutrons (uncharged subatomic particles). He produced neutrons by using the radiation from radioactive isotopes to bombard other atoms
Christopher Sydney Cockerell (1910–)	He invented the hovercraft, building the first working model in 1958
Sebastian Ziani de Ferranti (1864–1930)	He conceived the idea of the large-scale generation and distribution of high-voltage electricity, based on alternating current, and he established the concept of a national grid
Alexander Fleming (1881–1955)	In 1928 he discovered penicillin when he observed that the mould *Penicillium* produced an antibiotic substance that acted against a wide range of disease-causing bacteria. Penicillin was not, however, developed for use as an antibiotic drug until 1941
John Fleming (1849–1945)	He invented the thermionic valve in 1904 and was a pioneer in the application of electricity to lighting and heating on a large scale
Rosalind Franklin (1920–58)	She produced excellent X-ray diffraction pictures of DNA crystals which laid the foundations for the subsequent elucidation of the full chemical structure of DNA by James Watson and Francis Crick
Dennis Gabor (1900–79)	In 1947 he formulated the theory of holography, a photographic technique whereby a three-dimensional image of an object is produced. Holography was only achieved in practice after the development of the laser in the early 1960s
Stephen William Hawking (1942–)	He showed that black holes can radiate particles of matter, and he has made some of the most important discoveries about gravity since Einstein's theory of general relativity. He is currently working on a single theory that may explain the origin and structure of the universe, and he is well known for his best-selling account of modern cosmology, *A Brief History of Time* (1988)

Bradford Hill (1897–1991)	He introduced the application of rigorous statistical methods to the study of the distribution, effects, and causes of diseases in populations, and together with William Richard Doll he provided the first scientific evidence of a link between smoking and lung cancer in 1950
Arthur Holmes (1890–1965)	He determined the ages of rocks by measuring their radioactive constituents, and he was an early scientific supporter of the theory of continental drift
Frederick Hopkins (1861–1947)	He discovered 'accessory food factors', now known as vitamins, and established that they are essential for health
Godfrey Newbold Hounsfield (1919–)	He developed the technique of computer-assisted tomography (CAT), a diagnostic scanning technique used in medicine, whereby a clear image of internal structures in a single plane of a body tissue at a specified depth and angle is obtained
Mary Leakey (1913–)	In 1948 she discovered the skull of a prehistoric ape, *Proconsul africanus*, estimated to be 1.7 million years old, and in 1976 she led an expedition to Laetoli, Tanzania, where she found indisputable evidence that man's predecessors walked upright 3.75 million years ago
Bernard Lovell (1913–)	He initiated the establishment of the 250ft steerable radio telescope at Jodrell Bank (now Nuffield Radio Astronomy Laboratories), where he was director until 1981
Harry Moseley (1887–1915)	By means of X-ray spectra, he determined the atomic numbers of the chemical elements (Moseley's Law)
Clive Sinclair (1940–)	He launched his own electronics research and manufacturing company which developed and successfully marketed a wide range of pocket calculators, miniature television sets and personal computers. He later manufactured a small three-wheeled 'personal transport' vehicle (the 'C-5') powered by a washing-machine motor and rechargeable batteries
Alan Mathison Turing (1912–54)	He made important contributions to the design and programming of early electronic computers, and during World War II he devised the deciphering

	machine which broke the secret code of the German coding machine Enigma
Barnes Wallis (1887–1979)	He designed the Wellesley and Wellington bombers and the 'bouncing bombs' used during World War II by the Royal Air Force Dambusters Squadron
Robert Alexander Watson-Watt (1892–1973)	By 1935 he had developed the forerunner to radar, enabling aircraft to be located by detecting the echoes from a pulsed radio signal
Frank Whittle (1907–)	He patented the jet engine in 1930, and had developed the first successful prototype jet engine by 1937

SUMMARY OF EVENTS
1991–4

1991   Collapse of the Bank of Credit and Commerce International (BCCI): the Scottish Western Isles Council loses £24m as a result, and many individual investors are ruined

Gulf War: a war following the invasion of Kuwait by Iraq in Aug 1990. A rapid air and land campaign, code-named 'Desert Storm', is mounted by a US-led United Nations coalition. The most severe British losses during the war come when nine soldiers are killed by 'friendly fire' from a US aircraft after being wrongly identified. Iraqi forces are expelled from Kuwait and a large part of Iraq's military resources are destroyed

Scrapping of the Community Charge (Poll Tax) announced

The Queen makes her first visit to Northern Ireland in 14 years

Hostages John McCarthy and Terry Waite are released from Beirut after 1,943 and 1,763 days in captivity respectively

Helen Sharman, Britain's first female astronaut, embarks on an eight-day mission to the Russian space station MIR

Beginning of the Maastricht Summit to discuss European political and monetary union

1992   Conservative Party wins the General Election by 21 seats

The closure of Ravenscraig steel works is announced with the loss of 1,220 jobs

Foreign Secretary Douglas Hurd signs the Maastricht Treaty on European Union

An IRA bomb explodes outside the Baltic Exchange in the City of London, killing three people and causing £750m of damage. A second bomb explodes the next day at Staples Corner, London, also causing extensive damage

Media speculation about the marriage of the Prince and Princess of Wales is eventually followed by their separation

The Church of England synod approves the ordination of female priests

A fire at Windsor Castle results in £60m of damage

Two IRA bombings in Manchester injure 64 people

The Princess Royal (Princess Anne) marries Commander Timothy Laurence

Neil Kinnock resigns as leader of the Labour Party and is replaced by John Smith

The pound is effectively devalued following British withdrawal from the Exchange Rate Mechanism (ERM)

Summary of Events 1991–4

1993   Downing Street Declaration is made by the UK and Irish governments, outlining a structure for peace talks about the future of Northern Ireland

Ranulph Fiennes and Michael Stroud successfully complete the first unsupported crossing of the Antarctic on foot

An IRA bomb in Warrington kills two children and injures 56 others

The Queen and the Prince of Wales agree to pay income tax, capital gains tax and inheritance tax

Rebecca Stephens becomes the first British woman to climb Mount Everest

The Duke and Duchess of York announce their official separation

The British National Party (BNP) wins its first local council seat (Isle of Dogs, east London)

John Major launches his 'Back to Basics' campaign

The Lords and the Commons both vote in favour of the ordination of female priests

1994   A man fires a starting pistol at the Prince of Wales in Sydney, Australia, while the Prince is preparing to give a speech

Shops in Oxford Street, London, are seriously damaged after the explosion of IRA firebombs

The last major British-owned car manufacturer, Rover, is sold to German-owned BMW

A motion to reduce the age of consent for homosexuals to 16 is defeated by the House of Commons, but they do agree to lower it from 21 to 18

Ordination of the first female priests in the Church of England

Completion and opening of the Channel Tunnel: a tunnel from Cheriton near Folkstone in England to Sangette near Calais in France, begun in 1987. It consists of twin rail tunnels passing under the English Channel

Memorial services are held to commemorate the 50th anniversary of D-Day

The Scottish Episcopal Church votes to allow the ordination of female priests

Tony Blair is elected leader of the Labour Party following the death of John Smith

Establishment of the National Lottery

Index

Index

Index

Index

Index

Index

Index

Index

Index